T0279730

Saints of Switzerland

Claude Lopez-Ginisty

Translated from the French
by Archibald Andrew Torrance

Holy Trinity Publications
The Printshop of St Job of Pochaev
Holy Trinity Monastery
Jordanville, New York
2024

Printed with the blessing of His Grace,
Bishop Luke of Syracuse
and Abbot of Holy Trinity Monastery

PRINTSHOP OF
–SAINT JOB OF POCHAEV

An imprint of

HOLY TRINITY PUBLICATIONS
Holy Trinity Monastery
Jordanville, New York 13361-0036
www.holytrinitypublications.com

ISBN: 978-0-88465-495-7 (paperback)
ISBN: 978-0-88465-509-1 (ePub)

Library of Congress Control Number: 2024935681

Cover: "Church of St Martin, Zillis, Switzerland, 1980s." Source: jimfeng, scan
of film positive, istockphoto.com, ID 1343444140.

Printed in the United States of America

Dedication

In memory of St John of Shanghai,
who was the first to recommend
the veneration of the Orthodox Saints of Switzerland.

To Archbishop Anthony of blessed memory,
Archbishop of Geneva and Western Europe,
who encouraged Father Peter (the future Bishop
Ambrose) of Vevey to honor these Saints.

To Bishop Ambrose of Vevey, of blessed memory,
who composed the first service to all the Saints of Switzerland.

To Archbishop Michael of Geneva and Western Europe,
who entrusted me with this work and officially instituted
the Feast of All the Saints of Switzerland in his Diocese.

Fig 1 This icon, the *Synaxis of all the Saints of Switzerland*, was written at the Moscow Spiritual Academy in Sergiev Posad and is venerated in the Church of the Resurrection in Zurich, Switzerland.

Contents

PREFACE

What is most miraculous, is that the human race was converted by the very means which should rather turn them from faith in the Saviour: humiliations and torments, catacombs and the scaffold. Christ said: "And I, if I am lifted up from the earth, will draw all peoples to Myself" (John 12:32). His prophecy came true, but it was also fulfilled in the persons of the martyrs. Their deaths on their personal Calvaries proved to be the most effective preaching. Alongside each [martyr] Stephen we see a Saul becoming a St Paul, which led Tertullian to affirm "The blood of the martyrs is the seed of Christianity." We can see from this truth that what is most harmful to the Church is not the hatred of the impious, but the indifference of Her own children.

—CÉLESTIN DUBOIS,
Histoire des origines et de l'établissement
Du christianisme en Suisse,
[History of the Origins and Establishment
of Christianity in Switzerland]
Neuchâtel, 1859.

It could seem surprising that an Orthodox Christian should seek to make known the Western saints of the first millennium. Yet these saints belong to the Orthodox Church just as much as the Eastern saints; for they shared the same faith, the same spiritual life, and show us the same way to salvation. So those Orthodox, who had to flee their own countries after the tragic events of the Russian Revolution, came to breathe new life into the veneration of these saints, forgotten in the West and as yet unknown in the East. They fulfilled the famous prophecy of Ezekiel: "The hand of the Lord came upon me, and brought me by the Spirit of the Lord, and set me in the midst of the plain, which was full of human bones. . . .

and behold, there was a great multitude of bones on the face of the plain. They were very dry. Then He said to me, 'Son of man, can these bones live?' . . . I prophesied as He commanded me, and the Spirit entered into them; and they lived and stood upon their feet, an exceedingly great assembly" (Ezek 37: 1–10).

The first to breathe new life into this veneration was a contemporary Orthodox saint, the famous Archbishop John (Maximovitch, †1966), who was successively Archbishop of Shanghai, of Western Europe, and of Eastern America in the Russian Orthodox Church Outside Russia. Under his influence, this Church was the first to include the Western Orthodox saints in its canon.

A list of these saints, to be celebrated by the Church, was established by the Synod of Bishops of Western Europe, presided by Archbishop John (the future St John of Shanghai and San Francisco[1]) in Geneva on the 16th and 17th of September 1952. Among these saints were to be found some of the saints of Switzerland: Saints Columbanus, Gall, Fridolin, and Clotilde.

Then, with the blessing of Archbishop Anthony of Geneva and Western Europe, the priest of the parish of Lausanne-Vevey continued St John's work.

Several years ago, I was in the small house next to the Church of St Barbara in Vevey. I remember how both Fr Peter (Cantacuzène), later Bishop Ambrose, and Dr Barbara Heinz of blessed memory were poring over huge leather-bound volumes and translating passages from them. They were the *Lives of Swiss Saints* recorded in these ancient volumes in German Gothic. The bishop was taking notes for the service which he was then composing to the glory of all the holy enlighteners of Switzerland.[2] At the same time, he also commissioned Protodeacon George Jonneret of the Cathedral in Geneva to paint an icon of all these saints for the celebration of their feast.

When the service was completed and published, it was blessed by Metropolitan Vitaly, the First Hierarch of the Russian Church Outside Russia. It was celebrated at Vevey and the plans to transfer

Bishop Ambrose to South America were abandoned, to the great relief of his parishioners.

Bishop Ambrose was first bishop of Vevey (1993–2000), then bishop of Geneva and Western Europe (2000–2006). This left him little time to write the second part of the work which was to accompany the service to the saints: a synaxarion[3] containing short biographies of all the spiritual heroes of Orthodox Switzerland. Alas, the illness of our bishop led to his premature death. He was unable to apply himself to this work, and when he passed into heaven, he left behind nothing related to this pious endeavor in his papers.

I do not possess the encyclopedic knowledge of our late bishop, nor his deep understanding of both the history and hagiography of Switzerland. In this modest work, I start from the principles on which he composed his service to the saints and commissioned their icon.

This work would never have been undertaken had not Archbishop Michael of Geneva and Western Europe asked me to do so and encouraged me as I worked. In 2013, he came to the parish of Vevey to celebrate, in French,[4] the service composed by Archbishop Ambrose. He then issued an edict that all parishes in Switzerland should henceforth celebrate it every year on the third Sunday in September.[5]

Through my own research I have discovered saints who do not appear in the service of Archbishop Ambrose, or on the icon. But no synaxarion is ever truly complete. So some of the faithful will doubtless find other saints of whom I was unaware.

The choice of the Orthodox Saints featured in this collection is not arbitrary. They are the saints who lived before the Western schism of 1054. They confessed the Orthodox Faith and embraced no doctrine foreign to the teaching of the Fathers such as the *Filioque*. St Vincent of Lerins defined this perfectly in his *Commonitorium* (circa 428) "Take as the truth that which has been believed everywhere and at all times by everyone" (*Quod ubique, quod semper, quod ab omnibus creditum est*). For most of this work, we have followed the prudent limits for dating Orthodoxy set out by Charles Laporte in his fine work *All the Saints of Orthodoxy* (*Tous les saints de l'Orthodoxie*).[6]

In accordance with the Orthodox Tradition, we have chosen the date of *departure into heaven* (*dies natalis*) as the date for the feast wherever possible. Some lives are very short for lack of evidence. With the passage of time, many accounts of the lives have disappeared and only a name and a date remain. Others are longer and contain many details which may edify the faithful. But these things have no effect on the spiritual intercession and precious help which the saints afford us. Two anecdotes may help us to understand. One is from Mt Athos, and the other from the region of Zug in Switzerland:

One day, a monk had a vision of a wonderworking saint who was deeply venerated in his monastery. The saint said to him: "For many centuries you have venerated me with the name N . . . ; but this is not my name. Nevertheless you may continue to use this name." Then he disappeared without revealing his true identity; but his miraculous intercession continued.

At Cham, in the Canton[7] of Zug, a saint, whose name is unknown, has been venerated since the tenth century in the Church of St James. All we know is that after making a pilgrimage to the tombs of the Apostles in Rome, he stopped at Cham on the way back, and died. Some say he came from Scotland, others, from what is now Holland.

The names given to the saints may also vary according to the language used, but also according to the hagiographer. Thus in certain sources, St Theodoulos of Martigny is referred to as St Theodore, which is the tradition we follow in this work. Some saints are theognostics—known only to God—like the bishop at Cham referred to above. In any case, all those, who through the centuries have been glorified as saints, watch over us in the company of those elect ones known only to God. And we, the faithful of the Orthodox Church, find our spiritual roots as we discover our local saints.

The holy Archbishop John of Shanghai was the first to draw up a list of Western saints then unknown to the Russian Church, recommending, for example, the veneration of St Arsenios of Paros (†1877). He went on to declare one day: "The Church in the British Isles will only grow if she starts to venerate her own saints." These Western Orthodox saints are our roots in heaven. They join our Orthodoxy to the saints of the East whose churches gave us back the Faith of the Fathers: the Faith which our Western ancestors professed until the great schism.

Christianity was introduced gradually into Switzerland. As Celestin Dubois writes: "Our country is not vast. Yet six centuries were to pass before the Divine seed became widely rooted, spreading over those fields, rich in hope, to the delight of the Divine Harvester. The first rays of the Gospel shone beyond the Alps in the second century of our era, or possibly earlier. The last missionaries to work among us died around the end of the seventh or the beginning of the eighth centuries."[8]

There have been two kinds of invasion in the history of Switzerland. In the first, foreign peoples took over the land with the violence of their armies. They settled, and often mingled with the local population, mixing their beliefs with the pagan idolatry of the Swiss. There were also "missionary invasions," peaceful and spiritually fertile. They came from Frankish Gaul, from Ireland, and from the British Isles in general. There were also pilgrims who passed through Switzerland on their way to Rome, or on their return. As they progressed toward the tombs of the Apostles, they preached as they went.

Switzerland was pagan before its conquest by Caesar. It remained under Roman rule from 57 A.D. till 430 A.D. and parts became Christian. Then, from 430 A.D. until 550 A.D. it fell under the domination of the Allemans, the Burgundians, and the Ostrogoths who, in places, stained the Orthodox Faith with the Arian heresy. After this, the Franks ruled over the land from 550 A.D. until the eighth century.

> "Thus, in 550, after several centuries of trials and political change, Switzerland was once more united under a single scepter as she had been under the Romans. Her new masters divided the land into two parts. They attached to Swabia the part which had been

occupied by the Allemans, and all the areas where German was spoken: Raetia and the lands lying between lake Constance, the Rhine, the Aar, and St Gotthard.

The other parts, taken from the Burgundians [sic], where the main language was Roman [sic] were grouped into "Lesser Burgundy," or "Burgundy trans-Jura" with Orbe as its capital. This included Geneva, Vaud, the Valais, and parts of the modern cantons of Bern, Soleure, and Fribourg combined with Savoy. The German part was ruled by the Duke of Swabia or Allemania; the rest of the country by the Duke (or Viceroy) of Lesser Burgundy."[9]

What were the beliefs of the Swiss people when the Romans invaded their land? The Swiss worshiped the same gods as the Gauls. They were neighbors, so this was natural. There was Teutates (Toutatis), the equivalent of Mercury, who was patron of the favorite pastimes of the people. There was Belenus who personified the Sun (*Silva Belini,* now known as Sauvabelin, close to Lausanne, testifies to this cult). Hoesus, the equivalent of Mars, was the god of war. Taranus, or Taran, was their god of thunder, the equivalent of the Roman Jupiter. Penninus was the god of the heights in that majestic alpine scenery. Belisana, the mother of Belenus, was the goddess of water, of the arts, and of the hot springs. Apart from these, there were a host of other gods and goddesses who were linked to various activities of mankind and the forces of nature. Human sacrifice was not rare as a means of seeking the help of these gods!

The Allemans, who first invaded the Swiss lands in the second century, venerated Odin, or Wotan, whom they also called Allvitar (the father of all). They also venerated his wife, Hulda, the protector of homes, and his sons, Donat and Ziu, gods of tempest and of war, and Hertha, goddess of the Earth. They too sacrificed victims to the metallic idols of these gods.

The Burgundian invaders came from lands between the Vistula and the Oder. They had received basic Christian teaching, which was, alas, heretical, leaving them as followers of Arianism. One of their kings, St Sigismond, with most of his people, abandoned

Arianism for Orthodoxy at the Council of Saint-Maurice of Agaunum in 516. He it was who began the *perpetual prayer (laus perrennis)*, in Byzantine style, at the Monastery of Saint Maurice of Agaunum.

At the end of the first century, or the beginning of the second, it is highly likely that the first Christians appeared in Switzerland: Roman soldiers or Romanized Swiss. There were also preachers of the Gospel who came from Vienna. The Bishops of Vienna, Saints Paracode and Denis, encouraged this preaching. This explains why, jumping to conclusions, some have said that St Paracode was the first bishop of Geneva! Later, the coming of Celtic monasticism with St Columbanus, St Gall, and so many of their disciples was vital for the expansion of Christianity in Switzerland and its permanent rooting in the nation's soil.

For practical reasons, we have chosen to present the lives of the Orthodox saints of the Swiss lands as a synaxarion of the Church, arranged according to their dates, month by month, starting from September, the first month of the liturgical year. The dates cited are those of the civil (Gregorian) calendar followed by the civil date on the Julian Calendar used by most of the Orthodox Churches including the Russian Church.

The local Orthodox saints from every era are always with us and sometimes show their presence in extraordinary ways. Before the painting of the icon of all the saints of Switzerland, the parish of St Barbara in Vevey possessed a bas-relief on wood depicting them which had been carved by one of the parishioners. Close to the lower edge of this icon, there was a tiny reliquary containing a small fragment of the relics of the martyrs of Agaunum. When the painted icon was finished, the bas-relief was passed from one person to another until one day, it was noticed that it greatly pleased the Abbot of a Greek Monastery on Andros, a friend of our Russian Church and venerator of the Western Orthodox saints. It was taken to Greece and given to him.

The next year, some of the parishioners visited the island and saw some shiny spots on the bas-relief icon. Drawing near, they saw that these were drops of most fragrant myrrh which was coming from the images of St Beatus, St Maurice, and the martyrs of Agaunum, St Sigismond and St Clotilde. When asked about this, the abbot said that from time to time this fragrant oil flowed right down to the ground!

God is wonderful in His saints!

Saints of Switzerland, pray to God for us!

—Claude Lopez-Ginisty

St Tryphon 26th May 2014

Feast of saints Alexander of Rome, Glyceria and Laodicea, Alexander of Rome, Servais of Maastricht, Dominique of Côme, Maël the Welshman, Flaive of Châlons-sur-Saône, Dridan of Britanny, Natalis of Milan, Roland of Villiers-la-Poterie, John founder of the Monastery of Iveron on the Holy Mountain of Athos, Euthymios his son and George, abbot of the Monastery of Iveron, Onesimus Bishop of Soissons, Christiantien martyr of Ascoli, Rastagene martyr in Picardie, Agnes and Dioscole of Poitiers, Gwenganton of Vannes, Nicephoros of Aphasis, Pausicas of Synnades, Anno of Verona, Sergius confessor of the Holy Icons, Gabriel of Iveron who fetched the icon of the Portaïtissa from the sea, Euphrosynios of Iveron, Glyceria of Novgorod, the monks of Iveron martyred by the Latins (thirteenth century), Basil, Christopher, and Alexander martyrs of the communists, and all the other saints of the Church, known and unknown.

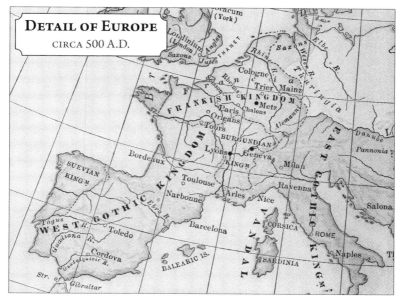

Fig 2 Detail of Europe in the reign of Theodoric circa 500 A.D.

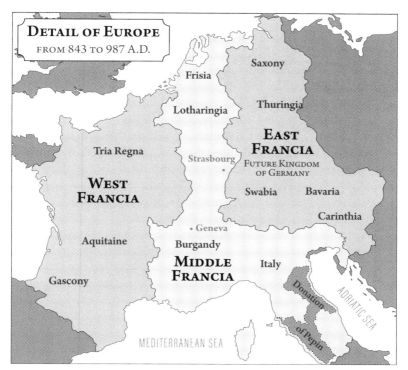

Fig 3 The Kingdom of Middle Francia was created in 843 by the Treaty of Verdun.

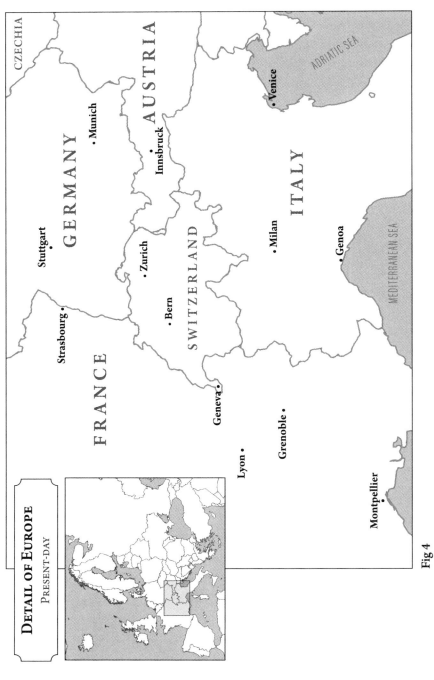

CZECHIA

GERMANY

• Munich

AUSTRIA

Stuttgart
•

Innsbruck
•

• Zurich

• Venice

ADRIATIC SEA

Strasbourg
•

SWITZERLAND

ITALY

FRANCE

• Bern

• Milan

• Genoa

MEDITERRANEAN SEA

Geneva •

Grenoble •

Lyon •

Montpellier
•

Fig 4

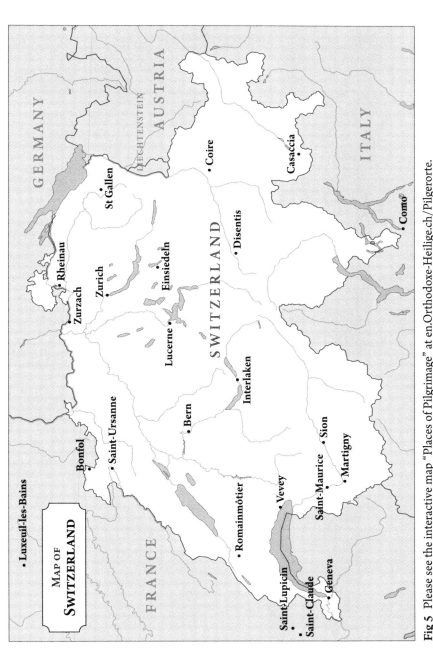

MAP OF
SWITZERLAND

• Luxeuil-les-Bains

GERMANY

AUSTRIA

LIECHTENSTEIN

ITALY

FRANCE

SWITZERLAND

• Coire

• Casaccia

• St Gallen

Como

• Rheinau

Zurzach

Zurich

• Einsiedeln

• Disentis

• Lucerne

Bonfol

• Saint-Ursanne

• Bern

• Interlaken

Sion

• Martigny

Saint-Maurice

• Vevey

• Romainmôtier

Saint-Lupicin

Saint-Claude

Geneva

Fig 5 Please see the interactive map "Places of Pilgrimage" at en.Orthodoxe-Heilige.ch/Pilgerorte.

SEPTEMBER

1ˢᵀ September / 14ᵀᴴ September

The Life of Our Mother among the Saints
Verena of Zurzach
(† Beginning of Fourth Century A.D.)
Feast day 1ˢᵗ September / 14ᵗʰ September.

Saint Verena came from Upper Egypt, the Thebaid, like the holy martyrs of Agaunum in the Valais. She lived at the end of the third and the beginning of the fourth centuries.

Verena went to Milan in the steps of the Theban Legion.[10] Learning of their massacre at Agaunum (now Saint-Maurice), she visited the place of their martyrdom. Afterwards, she withdrew to Solure where two soldiers of the legion, Ursus and Victor (who was said to have been her cousin), had been martyred. St Verena lived there as a hermit and cured several sick individuals who asked her for help. One of them was the Roman governor who had previously thrown her in prison and had her tortured for her preaching of Christ. Tradition related that whilst in prison, she had a vision of St Maurice who encouraged her to continue her evangelizing.

The saint left for Zurzach in the canton of Argovie, where her ascetic life of repentance and charity came to its end. Through her intercession many miracles have given glory to God.

A chapel was built over her tomb, and in the ninth century a double monastery, of nuns and monks, was founded.

She is one of the patrons of the diocese of Basel.

Saint Verena, pray to God for us!

Troparion of the Holy Martyr Saint Verena. Tone 6

Coming from Egypt like the Holy Legion, / and learning of its martyrdom, / thou didst make thy pilgrimage to Agaunum and Soleure / then didst withdraw from the world as a hermit in Zurzach. / In the ascetic life thou didst go forth to the Kingdom. / Saint Verena, pray to God that our souls may be saved.

1ˢᵗ September / 14ᵗʰ September

The Life of Our Father among the Saints
Audomar (or Omer) of Goldenthal
by Lake Constance
(†670 A.D.)
Feast day 1ˢᵗ September / 14ᵗʰ September.

Audomar was born in Goldenthal (the Golden Vale) by Lake Constance circa 600 A.D. His parents were Friulphe and Domitta. After his mother died, his father left the world and took Audomar with him to the monastery of St Columbanus at Luxeuil.

Audomar was tonsured a monk alongside his father by the Abbot Eustasius, and was ordained a priest. King Dagobert[11] appointed him Bishop of Noyon-Tournai (627–640 A.D.), and afterwards the Bishop of Théouanne (present-day Pas-de-Calais). There he preached to the Morins (Belgian Gauls) who had reverted to the darkness of paganism after the invasions of the Vandals[12] and the Sueves[13] in the fifth century. Audomar founded a monastery there where later the town of Saint-Omer (a variant of his name) was founded.

Close to the mouth of the river Aa dwelt Adrowald, a rich landowner who welcomed Audomar, gave him lodging, and was soon baptized into Christianity.

In 651, Adrowald gave Audomar several properties on the Aa including the Island of Sithiu. There he founded a church dedicated to the Mother of God, *Notre Dame*. He was assisted by three Benedictine monks: Mommelin, who was abbot of Sithiu before moving to Noyans; Bertin (his future successor), who founded the Church of St Peter—which later became the Abbey of St Bertin; and Bertrand of Cambrai, the future abbot of St Quentin.

Audomar went blind and reposed in 670 at Wavrans-sur-l'Aa. Respecting his last wishes, Bertin had his relics brought to the Church of Notre Dame in Sithiu. Though he "fought the good fight"[14] in distant lands, he is still numbered among the saints of Switzerland.

Saint Audomar, pray to God for us!

Troparion of Saint Audomar. Tone 4

Thou didst journey toward the Heavenly Kingdom, / first as a monk, then as a bishop, / and thou didst preach the Gospel of Jesus Christ to the peoples in heathen darkness. / Though Swiss thou becamest holy in foreign lands, / Saint Audomar, pray to God that our souls may be saved.

6ᵀᴴ September / 19ᵀᴴ September

The Life of Our Father among the Saints
Magnus (or Magnoald), Disciple of Saint Gall
(✝ 683 A.D.), Apostle to Italy, Switzerland, and Swabia.[15]
Feast day 6th September / 19th September

Little is known of Magnus other than that he was a disciple of St Gall and finished his earthly course in Swabia. According to tradition, his holiness was such that he had received power over animals as had Adam in Paradise.

St Columbanus predicted that Magnus would convert the people of the Julian Alps. After the death of this holy abbot, Magnus went to Kempten (Campidonum) to fulfill his holy master's prophecy. After his preaching was complete, he left to found the monastery of Füssen in 666 A.D.

St Magnus passed into heaven on 6th September 683 A.D.

Saint Magnus, pray to God for us!

Troparion of Saint Magnus, Shepherd and Martyr. Tone 3

Pious disciple of St Gall, / in the Swabian lands thou wast a perfect athlete of sobriety. / With worship, prayer, and fasting, / thou didst found the holy monastery of Füssen / before ascending peacefully to heaven. / Saint Magnus, pray to Christ our God that our souls may be saved!

11ᵀᴴ September / 24ᵀᴴ September

Life of the Holy Saints
Felix, Regula, and Exupery
(† Third Century).
Feast day 11ᵗʰ September / 24ᵗʰ September

According to tradition, Felix and Regula were brother and sister and both members of the Theban Legion who escaped the massacre of Agaunum. Maurice, the commander of the Legion, advised them to flee and they left before all other members of the Legion were martyred.

With their servant Exupery, they fled along the river Furka and over the Klausen Pass into the canton of Glaris. They finally reached Turicum (Zurich) where they were able to serve Christ. Soon they were discovered, and when under torture refused to worship the Roman gods. They were decapitated with their servant.

Holy Saints Felix, Regula, and Exupery, pray to God for us!

Troparion of Saints Felix, Exupery, and Regula. Tone 6

Enrolled in the holy Theban Legion, / who died for the Lord in the land of Agaunum, / ye left them before they passed into heaven./ Ye preached in the region of Zurich before being martyred in your turn./ Holy Saints of God, pray to Christ our God that He may save our souls!

12ᵀᴴ September / 25ᵀᴴ September and Friday after Ascension

The Life of Our Father among the Saints
Fromond
(Seventh Century)
Feast day 12ᵗʰ September / 25ᵗʰ September
and Friday after Ascension

Fromond was a hermit who lived at Bonfol in the Swiss Jura during the seventh century. According to legend, St Fromond, or Fromont (in Latin Fromundus or Frotmundus), was the son of a Norman king and a companion of St Ursanne (+ 620 A.D.) and of St Imier (+630–650 A.D.), who were both disciples of St Columbanus.

After leaving St Columbanus, these three monks went to dwell in the depths of the forests of the Jura. When they reached Mont-Repais at the summit of the Rangiers, each cast forth his staff and then departed in the direction his staff had fallen.

Fig 6 Seventeenth century ex-voto icon of Saint Fromond.

The staff of Ursanne fell beside the Doubs where there now stands the village of Saint-Ursanne. The staff of Imier fell toward the South, in the direction of the present village of Saint-Imier. Fromond followed his staff toward Ajoie and settled near a spring on the site which has since become the village of Bonfol in the Jura.

Fromond founded a hermitage beside this spring and planted his staff, which, as legend recounts, sprouted leaves and became the ancestor of the oaks which grow by the present-day village church.

People came to settle close to him, and he taught them the Gospel. As was the custom of the monks of that age, while toiling for the virtues of the soul to blossom he also cleared the surroundings for cultivation.

Fromond passed into heaven at the age of seventy. Today, there are many votive offerings of thanksgiving in his church, bearing witness to the miracles worked by the prayers of the saint.

Saint Fromond, pray to God for us!

Troparion to Saint Fromond the Hermit. Tone 6

A companion of St Ursanne and St Imier, /thou didst go with them to the desert of the Jura. / Then thou didst leave for Ajoie, / and beside a spring thou didst found a hermitage /wherein thou didst dwell until thy blessed passage into heaven. / Saint Fromond, pray to Christ our God to have mercy upon us!

13ᵀᴴ September / 26ᵀᴴ September

The Life of Our Father among the Saints

Amé

(570–625 A.D.), Monk of Saint Maurice of Agaunum, of Luxeuil, and of Remiremont, Abbot.
Feast day 13th September / 26th September

Saint Amé (570–625 A.D.) was born near Grenoble to a pious and noble Christian family of Roman heritage. From his childhood, he was especially disposed toward the Christian life. When he was ten years old, his pious father Heliodorus, took him to the monastery of Agaunum, which was famous throughout Gaul. Very quickly the boy's zeal for study and the monastic life was noticed. As soon as he was of age to pronounce his vows, he was received into the community.

The Acts of Saints (*Acta Sanctorum*) praise both his physical and spiritual qualities. It is said that he had "Holiness which all could see, charity which refused no one, and sober temperance …"

After thirty years in the community, Amé disappeared one morning from the monastery of St Maurice. The brotherhood searched for him everywhere and grew greatly concerned. As everyone began to fear the worst, they began to fast for him so that he might be protected.

Finally, the footprints of a man appeared in the snow close to the cliffs around the monastery. Following them they found Amé in a cave on a steep cliff, three hundred feet above the settlement. It is still there and is known as the cave of Scex above the village of Saint-Maurice, with a chapel full of votives built into the cliff. There was a mosaic icon of the saint affixed to the wall until recently, when it was unfortunately damaged by young vandals.

Fig 7 This seventeenth century wooden statue of St Amé de Remiremont was discovered in the cave known as the "Old Saint Amé", where, according to tradition, St Amé withdrew in sorrow for his sins, and to continue the ascetic struggle to purify his heart.

The pious Amé had come here to weep over his sins and to live as a hermit. He gave in to the kindness of his brothers, who understood his firm desire to live as a hermit, and accepted their offer of food every three days. A monk named Berin regularly brought him bread and water. Amé was moved by the faithful service of his brother and through a sense of charity wished to spare him so much effort. He asked him to draw near to the rock where his cave was set and to pray to the Lord that water might be given by God. After some time Amé arose, and thanking God, struck the rock with his staff. A pure and limpid stream of water gushed forth and continues to the present day.

He devoted himself to the main physical work of the monks of those days, clearing part of the forest next to his cave where he sowed barley. Thus, he could harvest his own grain and grind it with a crude mill to make flour for his bread.

Amé lived in ascetic labors and ceaseless prayer for three years. His fame was great and spread far beyond the bounds of the Valais. Circa 614, Eustaise, the successor to the great Columbanus at Luxeuil, heard of the saint and climbed the mountain to see him. Amazed by what he saw, he pressed him with pious arguments to come to Luxeuil. Amé yielded at last. When Eustaise returned from Bobbio and reminded him of his promise, Amé left his beloved cave and set out for Luxeuil, in 615.

At Luxeuil, the holy monk was admired by all. Eustaise decided to send him to tend to the needs of the Church. On one of his journeys, he met a rich and noble Christian who led a holy life. His name was Romaric, and he counted as lost any day in which he accomplished nothing for Christ. At the end of a meal, as is still the custom in the Orthodox Church, he asked this spiritual father to give him a word of salvation. Amé showed him a silver plate on the table. He told him that he was its slave, and that the apostle had said: "Your gold and silver are corroded, and their corrosion will be a witness against you and will eat your flesh like fire " (Jas 5:3).

The noble Romaric was moved by these words of the holy monk and asked him what he should do. Amé replied by reminding him of the story of the rich young man in the Gospel. So, Romaric sold all his goods and went to Luxeuil to be tonsured a monk.

Romaric kept back one property on which was a castle named Romariberg (later Remiremont) which he gave to Amé. Here, Amé founded a community of nuns with the blessing of Eustaise and many young girls came there to live under the rule of St Columbanus. The abbess he chose became St Macteflede. The community imitated the community of St Maurice of Agaunum, inspired by the unsleeping ones (*acemetes*) of St Marcel of Constantinople. Seven choirs, each of twelve sisters, took turns to maintain perpetual prayer in the church.

Wishing to found another community, the saint ordained Romaric abbot and started a community of monks on the same hill.

Amé himself remembered the solitary life of Scex at St Maurice. He longed for the days which he spent in pure prayer, communing in silence and holy solitude with God in the cave overlooking the Monastery of Agaunum. Amé found a cave on the slopes of Saint-Mont and dwelt there. He took up again his hermit life but continued to act as spiritual father with discernment and charity.

A monk who had left the Monastery of Luxeuil returned bearing an impious doctrine. When he came to Remiremont, God allowed Romaric and Amé to be deceived by the doctrine of this monk, and to stray from the Truth for a time. However, the intervention of St Eustaise and the ignoble death of this monk put the two fathers back on the right path. The account of this incident in the pious story of their life testifies to its truth.

Amé repented and redoubled his self-denial. He lived two further years of exemplary life and was then informed by God of his coming death. He asked a brother to fetch wood from the forest so that he could make a bed of cinders. Thus it was. A few days later, Amé put on his hair shirt, prostrated himself in the cinders, and confessed aloud all the sins he could remember. He then continued his repentance for a further year. Confined to bed, he received the brethren and gave them pious instruction. When he knew that death was at the door of his soul, he had the letter of St Leo, Pope of Rome to St Flavian read aloud. At each article of faith he said with a loud voice thus: "I believe" (*sic credo*). He died, confessing the Orthodox Faith, on 13th September / 26th September, 625.

Three days after his passage into heaven he appeared to a monk to say that he had found grace before God. He also predicted the future prosperity of Remiremont. A year later, he appeared again to ask that his relics be placed within the sanctuary of the Mother of God.

Two hundred years later, the relics of Saints Amé and Romaric were exhumed and found to be incorrupt, appearing as on the day of their death. Through their intercession, many miracles took place.

These two God-bearing fathers especially loved doves, which they used to feed. After their deaths, the monastery continued to feed the doves which gathered next to their tombs. When their relics were exhumed, these creatures could be seen escorting them as they flew. The doves entered the holy place and made their nests in the roof, and for four hundred years faithfully guarded the holy relics.

The miracles continued abundantly, witnessing to the holiness of these pious monks. Among these miracles of their intercession is the case of a child whose eyelids were sealed together, and who saw light after they were anointed with oil from the lamp which burned before the tomb of St Amé.

During the French Revolution the relics were profaned and scattered over the sacristy of the church. Some of them were saved by the nuns, who returned them to the church once the tempest had passed. However, the community of Remiremont, founded by St Amé, did not survive the senseless and impious fury of the revolutionaries.

Saint Amé, pray to God for us!

Troparion of Saint Amé of Agaunum. Tone 4

Thou didst live from thy childhood in a holy monastery / which sheltered the relics of the martyrs of Agaunum. / Thou didst climb to the cave of Scex to live as a hermit, / before going to Luxeuil and Remiremont to found new communities. / Saint Amé, pray to Christ our God to have mercy upon us.

22ND SEPTEMBER / 5TH OCTOBER

The Life of Our Fathers among the Saints
Maurice and Those with Him at Agaunum
(† 285–286 A.D.)
Feast day 22nd September / 5th October

At the time when Maximinian[16] shared the Roman Empire with Diocletian,[17] there was in the Roman army a Legion made up soldiers coming from Thebes in Egypt which was sent to the West to reinforce Maximinian's troops. There were 6,600 men in this Legion; all were fine warriors, distinguished by their "magnanimous courage" in combat "and by a faith still more magnanimous."[18] The Legion rendered faithfully "to God the things that are God's" and to "Caesar the things that are Caesar's." (Mark 12:17).They were ordered to search out the Christians and to bring them before the emperor. The Legion refused, saying that they could not obey such orders. Maximinian came to Octodurum (now Martigny) at the approach to Entremont on the Dranse. When he was told that a legion, stationed at Tarnade (afterwards Agaunum), had rebelled and refused his orders, he flew into a rage. Burning with anger, he ordered that it should be decimated, thinking that terror would persuade some to yield to his will and fulfill his impious plans.

Immediately after the first executions, he renewed his orders that those who were left alive should pursue the Christians. As soon as the Theban Legion heard this new order, they all cried out that in no way would they participate in this impious deed, and would suffer anything rather than betray their Christian Faith. Their reply made Maximinian crueler than a wild beast. He ordered that they should be decimated again and be obliged to submit to the law. When this bloodthirsty command arrived in their camp the second time, the soldiers of Christ remained unbending in their resolution, and a tenth of the remaining soldiers were massacred. But those who were spared death encouraged each other to persevere in their resolve.

Among these heroes of the Faith in Switzerland were St Maurice, their commander, St Exupery, the adjutant of the camp, and Candide, the provost of the troops.

Saint Maurice urged them all to remain firm in their faith, giving them their comrades in arms as examples of those who had gone to join the heavenly army of Christ. They sent a deputation to Maximinian with this message:

> O Emperor, we are your soldiers, but it is also our glory to confess aloud that we are servants of God. To you we owe our military service; to Him the homage of an innocent life. From you we receive the wages of our work and our labours; from Him the gift of life. This is why, O Emperor, we cannot obey you if by this we were to deny our God, Creator of all. He is our Master and our Creator, and yours as well, whether you will or no. Refrain from imposing on us the unhappy duty of offending Him, and you will find us to be, as always, ready to follow your orders. Otherwise, know that we will obey Him rather than you. Our arms are ready against whatever enemy you would strike down, but it would be a crime to soak them with the blood of innocents. These hands know how to fight our enemies and the impious; but they cannot cut the throats of the friends of God and our brothers. We have not forgotten that it was to protect our fellow citizens, not to strike them down, that we took up arms. We have always fought for justice, for piety and for the salvation of innocents. In the midst of dangers, we have never sought any other reward. We have fought respecting our oath to you; but how can we keep it if we abjure our oath to God ? Our first oaths are sworn to God, and only then to you. We cannot remain faithful to our oath to you if we abjure the former. You order us to seek out Christians to be punished; but we ourselves are Christians. Here we are: your wish is fulfilled. You have no need to seek out others. Before you are men who confess God the Father, Maker of all things, and who believe in

Jesus Christ, His Son, as God. We have seen our comrades, who shared our labors and perils, fall beneath the sword, and we were sprinkled with their blood. Yet we did not weep over our blessed brothers' death in this cruel massacre; nor did we bewail their lot. Instead, we were glad for their happiness, and we accompanied their sacrifice with feelings of joy, for they were found worthy to suffer for their Lord and their God. As for us, we are not rebels who are in revolt through the need to live. We have not taken up arms against you through despair, so powerful in danger. We have our weapons in our hands, but we will not resist. We would rather die than kill, to perish in innocence rather than live in guilt. If you decree further laws against us, if you pronounce new sentences of fire, torture, or the sword we will not be afraid. We are ready to die. We proclaim with a loud voice that we are Christians and that we cannot persecute Christians.[19]

Maximinian understood their steadfastness and the firmness of their faith and decided to massacre the whole legion at once and the glorious Theban Legion died without a murmur for the Christian Faith. The earth was bestrewn with the corpses of the holy victims and their innocent blood flowed in long streams. Thus perished that truly angelic legion.

The bodies of the martyrs of Agaunum were discovered, after a revelation, by St Theodore,[20] Bishop of Martigny in the Valais. He had a basilica built in their honor, set against an enormous rock. There people came to venerate the holy relics of the soldiers of Christ. Miracles illumined their heavenly glory ceaselessly, showing forth signs of the Grace of God, in countless healings and conversions. The veneration of the holy martyrs spread like a wave through the Christian world as the many cities named after the martyr St Maurice attest.

Some of the soldiers of the Legion escaped the massacre and became missionaries of the Gospel. They also died martyrs to the Faith and can be found at Soleure and elsewhere in Switzerland.

St Martin,[21] the great bishop, bears witness of the fervor with which the holy martyrs of Agaunum were venerated in his day. He was most devoted to these glorious martyrs and traveled to

Agaunum to seek some relics. After he was refused by the monks who dwelt there, he traveled on to the place where they had died—Verolliez (i.e., "the true place" of the martyrdom close to the Rhone). Once there, after fervent prayer, he took a knife and cut sod from the earth in the form of a crown. Straight away blood flowed out abundantly which he collected in a vase brought for that purpose. He left some of the blood at Agaunum with the knife, and took the rest to Tours. There he divided it among several churches, mostly in his own cathedral and that of Angers. He kept a small vial of it for himself which he always carried and with which he desired to be buried.

Recently, the abbot of a monastery of the Patriarchate of Moscow in Western Europe had a square sod of the earth of the martyrs cut out and transferred it to his monastery.

Saint Maurice is the patron saint of soldiers. They invoke him, alongside St George, that through their prayers they may be granted victory.

Saint Maurice and all the holy martyrs of Agaunum, pray to God for us!

Troparion of Saint Maurice of Agaunum. Tone 4

O soldier of Christ, / thou didst fight the good fight, refusing to pursue the innocent. / And thou gavest thy life / with the lives of thy companions rather than renounce thy Christian Faith. / O Saint Maurice, / pray to the Lord that He may grant us His great mercy!

22ᴺᴰ SEPTEMBER / 5ᵀᴴ OCTOBER

The Life of Our Father among the Saints
Antoninus of the Theban Legion
(† 285/286 A.D.)
Feast day 22ⁿᵈ September / 5ᵗʰ October

Saint Antoninus was martyred with St Maurice and his companions at Agaunum. He is especially honored in Plaisance and in the Church of St Victrix in Rouen where his relics were sent by St Ambrose of Milan.[22]

Saint Antoninus, pray to God for us!

Troparion of Saint Antoninus. Tone 4

Soldier of Christ in the Theban Legion, / thou didst suffer martyrdom with thy companions, / and thy holy relics were sent by the great Saint Ambrose / to the Church of Gaul where they worked great miracles. / Saint Antoninus, / pray to Christ our God to save our souls.

28ᵀᴴ SEPTEMBER / 11ᵀᴴ OCTOBER

The Life of Our Father among the Saints
Salonius of Geneva
(Fifth Century)
Feast day 28ᵗʰ September / 11ᵗʰ October

Saint Salonius was born in 405 A.D. His father was St Eucher of Lyon, his mother was named Galla, and his brother was St Veran of Vence. Around 415, St Salonius went with his family to live on the isles of Lerins where St Honorat had just founded his famous monastic community.

He was educated by Saints Salvian, Vincent of Lerins and Hilarion who was later Bishop of Arles. Saint Salonius's father lived for some years as a hermit in the Luberon before being consecrated

Metropolitan of Lyon. He took part in the Council of Orange in 441 with Salonius, who had been a monk in Lerins before being consecrated Bishop of Geneva. Salonius also took part in the Council of Vaison in 442 and in the Council of Arles in 451.

Saint Eucher dedicated to him his "Instructions to Salonius, Book II" (*Instructionum ad Salonium, libri II*), which are commentaries on biblical texts. His former tutor, St Salvian, dedicated to him the work he published circa 439: "On the Government of God" (*De gubernatione Dei*). We possess few other details of his life and do not know the date of his death.

Several biblical commentaries and dialogues are attributed to St Salonius in which he replies to the questions of his brother St Veran on the moral teaching of the books of Proverbs and Ecclesiastes: *Mystical Exposition on the Parables of Solomon and Ecclesiastes* (*Expositio Mystica in Parabolas Salomonis et in Ecclesiasten*).

Saint Salonius, pray to God for us!

Troparion of Saint Salonius of Geneva. Tone 4

At the age of ten thou didst depart to Lerins / to work under the guidance of Saint Honorat, / with Saints Hilarion and Vincent for teachers. / As hierarch of the town of Geneva, / thou didst govern the Church with great wisdom. / Saint Salonius, / pray to Christ our God to save our souls.

30ᵀᴴ SEPTEMBER / 13ᵀᴴ OCTOBER

The Lives of Our Fathers among the Saints
Ursus and Victor
(† circa 286/288 A.D.)
Feast day 30th September / 13th October

Both Saints Ursus (Ours) and Victor were soldiers of the Theban legion decimated at Agaunum (as described in the previous life of St Maurice). Both left for Soleure before the massacre of the martyrs of Agaunum (present-day Saint-Maurice in the Valais).

They were arrested there by the governor and condemned to be burnt alive since they would not sacrifice to the false gods of the Romans. However, a violent thunderstorm and heavy rains extinguished their pyre. Histacus, the governor then, had the saints beheaded beside the river Aar. Their heads and bodies fell into the water, but "swam" miraculously to a bay where the Christians recovered them and gave a Christian burial.

Their holy relics, which were once shared between the monastery of St Victor in Geneva and Soleure are now at rest in the cathedral of St Ursus in Soleure.

Saints Ursus and Victor, pray to God for us!

Troparion of Saints Ursus and Victor. Tone 6

Escaping from the Theban Legion in Agaunum / ye departed to preach Christ to those who lay in pagan darkness. / Taken by the tyrant and condemned to death, / ye were martyred beside the river Aar. / Saints Ursus and Victor, / pray to Christ our God to save our souls.

OCTOBER

2ᴺᴰ October / 15ᵀᴴ October

The Life of Our Father among the Saints
Ursicin, Abbot of the Monastery of Disentis, then Bishop of Coire
(✝ 760 A.D.)
Feast day 2ⁿᵈ October / 15ᵗʰ October

Little is known of St Ursicin (Ursicinus): he was a monk, then Abbot of the Monastery of Disentis in Switzerland, and later became Bishop of Coire. Attracted by the solitary life, he resigned his episcopacy in 758 and retired to a hermitage in the area where he passed into heaven on 2ⁿᵈ October / 15ᵗʰ October 760.

Saint Ursicin, pray to God for us

Troparion of Saint Ursicin. Tone 4

Thy life was hidden from the gaze of the world; / thou didst dwell in prayer and abstinence in God. / Thou wast a monk of the Monastery of Disentis / before ruling the see of Coire. / Resigning thy see / thou becamest a hermit. / Saint Ursicin, pray to Christ our God to save our souls.

12ᵀᴴ OCTOBER / 25ᵀᴴ OCTOBER

The Life of Our Father among the Saints

Pantalus, Bishop and Martyr of Basel

(† circa 453 A.D.)

Feast day 12ᵗʰ October / 25ᵗʰ October

Saint Pantalus, or Pantale, was the first Bishop of Basel in Switzerland and gained heaven through martyrdom. His life is linked to the traditions surrounding St Ursula and her companions.

He most likely accompanied them to Rome and, as they returned, was martyred with them by the Huns in Cologne on 12ᵗʰ October / 25ᵗʰ October circa 453.

His relics were placed in the Cathedral of Cologne, apart from his precious head, which was given to the Cathedral of Basel. There it was venerated until it disappeared during the impious profanations and plundering which took place during the Reformation.

Saint Pantalus, pray to God for us!

Troparion of Saint Pantalus. Tone 4

Thou wast the first hierarch of the city of Basel, / and didst accompany St Ursula and her companions / as they made their pilgrimage to the city of Rome. / Returning, thou wast martyred / in Cologne, with the virgins of St Ursula's company. / Holy Father Pantalus, pray to Christ our God to save our souls!

16ᵀᴴ OCTOBER / 29ᵀᴴ OCTOBER

The Life of Our Father among the Saints
Gall, Monk and Abbot
(+ 646 A.D.)
Feast day 16th October / 29th October

Saint Gall was the most famous disciple of St Columbanus, and was born around the middle of the sixth century in Ireland. From his childhood, he was placed by his parents in the Monastery of Bangor where he was educated by Saints Comgall and Columbanus. The monastery was celebrated for its school whose excellence rivaled the great piety of its monks. The young Cellach, who was to become St Gall, became an expert in poetry and Holy Scripture.

Fig 8 St Gall

Saint Columbanus judged him worthy of the great and awesome rank of priesthood and ordained him. After many years of ascetic labors, he was chosen by the saint, with the blessing of St Comgall,[23] as one of the twelve monks to accompany him beyond the green coasts of Ireland to preach the Word of God. St Columbanus and his twelve disciples went first to England. Then, circa 585, they proceeded to France. Thanks to the good will of a Frankish king, they settled at Annegray in the Vosges where they founded a monastic community. The grace resting on the Abbot, Columbanus, drew many disciples to the place.

Around 590, Saints Columbanus and Gall founded a new community in Luxeuil, a spa town which had been completely destroyed by the Huns. An old house in ruins was converted to a

S GALLÆ PANE PORRIGIT VRSO

Fig 9 Ivory plate sculpted by St Tutilon (see page 72), from the cover of the *Evangelium Longum*. St Gall is depicted: sleeping by the fire; being helped by a bear to build his cell; and handing the bear a loaf of bread.

chapel and then a monastery. Once again, the manifest holiness of the abbot attracted new disciples who came to the brotherhood.

The monastery grew and the monks were numerous. As the chronicle relates, the place became so famous that King Thierry, the son of King Childebert (circa 496 – †13 December 558) often came to visit St Columbanus and his disciples. But the abbot was no hypocritical flatterer of the great ones of this world. He rebuked King Thierry continuously for the way he despised his true wife and indulged in adulterous love with his concubines.

Thierry had great respect for the holy monk which greatly alarmed his grandmother, Brunehaut.[24] She saw how much he honored St Columbanus and feared that he might follow his holy advice, chasing away his concubines and living faithfully with his wife. Her power, as queen mother, would be seriously impaired by the return of her daughter-in-law.

She decided to exile St Columbanus and ordered him to leave the kingdom. He did, taking with him St Gall, his companion in all his joys and sorrows, and several other monks.

They left for Austrasia, then ruled by Theodebert from his capital in Metz. Together they traveled all through Germany, suffering a thousand sorrows and a thousand persecutions. "As soon as they had settled in a place," relates the chronicle, "the Evil One, who knew what he had to fear, incited folk to chase them away to another place." In the end, the pious Villemar, a priest of Arbonne by Lake Constance, provided them with a place to withdraw at Bregenz. There they built cells, and at once began to convert the pagans of the place. They even persuaded them to break up their idols and to throw the pieces into the lake.

Two monks were martyred by those pagans who remained in the darkness of ignorance. Their bodies were placed beneath the altar of the Abbey of Angia Major, or Brigantina, in Swabia, which was later called Mererau.

When Thierry slew Theodebert in battle, he became king of Austrasia. Afterwards, St Columbanus decided to depart into Italy and asked St Gall to go with him, but St Gall was very sick and asked to be left at Bregenz. This illness prevented him, for the first time, from obeying and following his spiritual father. The chronicle relates that St Columbanus, who was resolved to complete this journey, allowed him to remain in Bregenz and left him in his peace; however, he enjoined him never again to celebrate the divine liturgy whilst St Columbanus was still alive.

Saint Columbanus departed for Italy around 612. After his health was restored, St Gall moved further up the lake with several companions and built new cells. These developed into the Monastery of St Gall, as it later came to be known.

He learned the language of the region and converted so many idolators that he became known as the "Apostle of Constance." Saint Gall also worked many miracles and healings. The daughter of Duke Gouzon (or Gunzon) was possessed, and the good saint delivered her from the demon. Afterwards, the duke wished to appoint him to a bishopric. St Gall refused, as always, any honors and authority in the Church. The chronicle also relates that the duke wished to give him much gold, something the saint could not refuse. But St Gall soon disposed of it by giving it to the poor. When a deacon showed him a vessel which he wished to keep for the service of the altar St Gall replied: "No, do not keep it. We must be able to say, with St Peter, 'Silver and gold I do not have' (Acts 3:6)."

After matins on the day of a great feast, it was revealed to St Gall that his Holy Father Columbanus had just died. He alerted the community, and they celebrated the funeral office. Then he sent one of his monks to verify the facts. The monk returned with a letter from the monks of St Columbanus confirming his death. It explained that before dying, he had expressed the wish that his abbot's staff should be given to St Gall as a sign that he was absolved of his failure to follow him to Italy.

Saint Gall shed floods of tears, for he had never ceased loving his father Columbanus. He had obeyed him by never celebrating the Divine Liturgy right up to that moment as his master had instructed and had refused the bishoprics which men wished to force upon him. In this way his Holy Father Columbanus had preserved him in that arduous monastic life so dear to the Irish monks.

Saint Gall never left his cell other than to preach the Gospel. He devoted himself to the instruction of the humblest and most miserable of men, and then retired to his cell. Like our father among the saints St Seraphim of Sarov, he had befriended a bear which often visited him and sometimes brought him firewood! This bear is commemorated to this day in the coat of arms of the town of Saint-Gall as a memorial to the holy hermit. Also, like St Seraphim, he passed his days and nights in ardent prayer and in constant meditation on the word of God.

The chronicle relates that the pious King Sigisbert (also a saint, commemorated on 1ˢᵗ February / 14ᵗʰ February and who founded many monasteries) had a great veneration for St Gall. His daughter refused marriage so as to become a nun close to his monastery.

In 625, St Eustaise the Abbot of Luxeuil died. His monks chose St Gall as his successor. But the Monastery of Luxeuil had become too wealthy and our holy father feared riches like the plague. There were also very many monks, and St Gall refused and remained in his hermitage.

Saint Gall directed his monks according to the strict rule of St Columbanus. This most austere monastic rule was based on perfect obedience, silence, fasting, and abstinence. Attached to it was a code of severe penances for any infraction of the monastic rule.

The only writing of St Gall which has come down to us is a sermon preached on the consecration of his disciple, John, to the episcopate. The see was first proposed to St Columbanus, who refused it and recommended John, his deacon. John was unanimously elected to the bishopric. The text of this sermon can be found in the "Ancient Lessons" (*Lectiones Antiquae*) of Canisius.[25]

Saint Gall died after a short illness on 16th October / 29th October 646. The chronicle mentions that he had reached the venerable age of ninety-five. This chronicle, supported by other ancient documents, is the source of this life. It was written by Vualfrid (or Walafride), nicknamed Strabo ("the squint-eyed"), a monk of the Monastery of St Gall, who later became abbot of a monastery in the diocese of Constance. He died in 849, around two centuries after the death of St Gall. It was in the Monastery of St Gall that he collected the pious recollections of his life.

Saint Gall, pray to God for us!

Troparion of Saint Gall. Tone 8

A disciple of Saint Columbanus who came to Gaul, / thou didst found with him the Abbey of Luxeuil, /but when he departed in exile for Italy, /thy sickness kept thee back by Lake Constance, / where thy hermitage became a monastery. /Saint Gall, pray to Christ our God to have mercy upon us.

NOVEMBER

2ND NOVEMBER / 15TH NOVEMBER

The Life of Our Father among the Saints
Ambrose I, Abbot of Agaunum
(†516–523 A.D.)
Feast day 2nd November / 15th November

Saint Ambrose was Abbot of the Monastery of Ile-Barbe in Lyon, the first monastery on French soil. He was then called to succeed Ynnemod, the Abbot of Agaunum in the days when King Sigismond lived there in repentance for the sin of murdering his son. The tradition relates that he was called to this noble office on account of his excellent reputation in clerical circles.

He had the gift of prophecy and composed a famous prayer to Christ and His Most Pure Mother. He also started the perpetual prayer (*laus perennis*) in this famous monastery of the Valais. Finally, he repaired the damage caused by those who seized King Sigismond from the Abbey by force.

Saint Ambrose, pray to God for us!

Troparion of Saint Ambrose I. Tone 4

Abbot of the Monastery of Ile-Barbe, / the first monastery in the land of Gaul. / Thou wast called in the days of King Sigismond

/ to lead the community of Agaunum. / There thou didst ordain perpetual prayer. / Holy Father Ambrose, pray to God to save our souls.

3ᴿᴰ NOVEMBER / 16ᵀᴴ NOVEMBER

The Life of Our Father among the Saints

Pirmin, Abbot, Founder of Reichenau and Murbach, and a Local Bishop

(† 753 A.D.).

Feast day 3ʳᵈ November / 16ᵗʰ November

Pirmin is said to have come from France. He left his parents while still young to devote himself to preaching and the priesthood and founded a mission center in Meltis Castle (village of Medelsheim) in the Deux-Ponts region of the diocese of Spire. Later, two leagues (approximately 11 kilometers) away, Pirmin founded the famous Abbey of Hornbach around 740.

From Meltis, Pirmin set out on his apostolic missions. Around 723, a German nobleman, Syntlaz, called him to preach in some of the provinces bordering the Rhine. In Switzerland, Pirmin's preaching of the Word of God and the Gospel of the Kingdom of Heaven met with success, and Syntlaz asked him to found a monastery on his lands.

Pirmin chose an island in the Rhine close to Constance where he founded the Monastery of Reichenau which became famous for its riches. Before its foundation, he drove away all the serpents which previously had infested the island.

Pirmin's fame was esteemed by Charles Martel (Mayor of the Palace[26] and ruler of Frankia); but this provoked the jealousy of the German dukes, obliging him to leave his monastery and settle in Alsace. There, supported by the authority and generosity of Charles Martel, he, with benevolent zeal, founded many monasteries in the provinces along the Rhine. The rest of his life was spent visiting various monasteries and restoring their discipline.

Pirmin fell asleep in peace in the Lord the 3rd of November / 16th November 758.

Saint Pirmin, pray to God for us!

Troparion to Saint Pirmin. Tone 4

Thou didst found the famous Monastery of Hornbach / and didst preach the Gospel along the banks of the Rhine. / Thou didst continue thy mission in Switzerland, / and on an island in the Rhine didst found Reichenau. / Thou wast a preacher full of zeal for the Faith. / Holy Father Pirmin, pray to Christ our God to save our souls.

6ᵗʰ November / 19ᵗʰ November

The Life of Our Father among the Saints
Protais (Protase or Prex) Bishop of Lausanne
(Middle of Seventh century)
Feast day 6th November / 19th November

Little is known of his life. Protais was Bishop of Lausanne around the middle of the seventh century during the reign of Clovis II, King of the Franks (633–657). First as a priest, then as a bishop, he practiced self-denial and charity.

He enlarged the Chapel of Saint Thyrse and dedicated it to St Maure. With the backing of Felix, Duke of Burgundy, and his wife Ermentrude, he built the Church of Baulmes and its monastery dedicated to the Mother of God. He was authorized to use the timber from the forests of Mount Tendre in the Jura to rebuild the Church of Lausanne, but there he had a fatal accident. While helping with the felling he died tragically when a tree fell on him.

His body was laid to rest in the Church of Basuges. Since it proved impossible to move the holy relics of the bishop, it was seen that it was God's will that they should rest where they were buried until the day of the general resurrection.

The saint gave his name to the village of Saint-Prex. Once called Saint-Protase (from the Latin *Sanctus Protasius*), the name evolved to Saint-Prothais, then Saint-Pré, and finally to Saint-Prex, the present name. His relics repose in the church of this village which once was called Basuges.

Saint Protais, pray to God for us!

Troparion of Saint Protais, Bishop of Lausanne. Tone 5

Humble hierarch devoted to thy diocese, / thou didst lead a pious life hidden in God. / Coming from Burgundy into Switzerland, / and rebuilding the Church of Lausanne, / thou didst go to the Lord in His Kingdom. / Saint Protais, pray to Christ our God that he may save our souls.

8ᵀᴴ November / 21ˢᵀ November

The Life of Our Father among the Saints
Gregory, Abbot of Einsiedeln
(✝ 996 A.D.)
Feast day 8th November / 21st November

Gregory was a member of one of the royal families of England who left his wife, with her consent, to enter the Monastery of Mount Coelius in Rome. From there he went to the famous Benedictine Abbey of Einsiedeln, still known as *Notre Dame des Ermites* (Our Lady of the Hermits) where he became abbot. According to tradition, it was a vision of an angel which led him to go there.

When he died, on 8th November / 24th November 996, he was buried next to the altar of St Maurice of Agaunum, and many miracles took place at his tomb.

Saint Gregory, pray to God for us!

Troparion of Saint Gregory. Tone 5

Leaving thy noble rank in Albion's Isle, / thou wast professed a monk in the City of Rome, / whence thou didst depart at last to Einsiedeln. / There thou wast elected abbot for thy great piety, / and thy holy relics worked miracles. / Holy Father Gregory, pray to Christ our God to save our souls.

13ᵗʰ November / 26ᵗʰ November

The Life of Our Father among the Saints

Imier (or Hymier)

(† circa 620 A.D.)
Feast day 13th November / 26th November

Saint Imier (Hymier, Imerius) was born around 570 at Lugnez, near Porrentruy. He came from a distinguished family and from his childhood was drawn to prayer and solitude in God. Imier spent time in Lausanne and made a pilgrimage to the Holy Land where he was ordained a priest by the Patriarch of Jerusalem, Isaac.[27] He returned to the valley of the Duze to work out his salvation.

Soon, many monks gathered around him. He built a church dedicated to St Martin of Tours for the community which had sprung up.

After guiding his companions on the way of salvation, St Imier fell asleep in Christ on 13th November / 26th November 620. At his tomb, and through his intercession, many miracles took place.

Saint Imier, pray to God for us!

Troparion of Saint Imier. Tone 6

Thou didst leave this vain world to draw close to God. / From thy childhood thou didst desire the treasures of heaven. / Coming to Jerusalem as a pilgrim, / the Patriarch ordained thee a priest. / Returning home thou didst take other monks under thy wing. / Saint Imier, pray to Christ our God to save our souls.

13ᵗʰ November / 26ᵗʰ November

The Life of Our Father among the Saints
Fintan (sometimes called Findan), Monk then Recluse

(✝ 878 A.D.)
Feast day 13ᵗʰ November / 26ᵗʰ November

Fintan came from noble Irish stock of Leinster in the ninth century. He lost his parents, brothers, and sisters to the conflicts between Irish clans and to Viking raids. He himself was captured and taken by the Vikings to the Orkneys, but managed to escape and flee to Scotland. Fintan stayed there two years with a bishop and then in 845 made a pilgrimage through France to Rome where he venerated the tombs of the Apostles.

He was a monk at Farfa in Italy and then left for Swabia where, as a priest, he became the chaplain of a German noble. After several years, in 851, he entered the Monastery of Rheinau on Lake Constance (Bodensee) as a monk. From 856 until his death in 879 he lived in self-denial and prayer, enclosed in his cell as a recluse.

His holy relics are preserved in the church of the Monastery of Rheinau.

Saint Fintan, pray to God for us!

Troparion of Saint Fintan. Tone 7

Son of noble Irish blood, thou didst lose all thy family and became a slave. / Escaping from captivity thou didst flee to Scotland / and wast a pilgrim in Italy and Swabia before becoming a recluse in Switzerland. / Holy Father Fintan, pray to Christ our God to save our souls.

16ᵀᴴ November / 29ᵀᴴ November

The Life of Our Father among the Saints

Othmar, Abbot of Saint Gall

(† 759 A.D.)

Feast day 16ᵗʰ November / 29ᵗʰ November

The life of St Othmar was written by Walafrid Strabo, the Abbot of Reichenau († 849). At first it was just an appendix to the life of St Gall, but later it was enlarged into a special biography by Deacon Gozbert[28] around 830.

When St Gall refused to follow his abbot (St Columbanus), he wished to live as a hermit in stable conditions. When he died, he was buried on the spot. His tomb was at once venerated as the tomb of a saint, and a church was built around which dwelt hermits who followed the rule of St Columbanus.

Around 720, Othmar, then the abbot, introduced the rule of St Benedict which transformed the colony of hermits into a monastery. It grew to great importance during the following century.

Othmar was born in Thurgovia and educated at the court of Victor, the Count of Coire. After his ordination he was placed in charge of a church dedicated to St Florinus (†856). A nobleman named Waltram claimed hereditary rights over the lands of Saint-Gall, and asked Count Victor to permit Othmar to lead the hermits. In Othmar's day, the buildings were certainly modest, since they all had to be rebuilt at the beginning of the following century. The charter's extant shows that extra lands were granted to the monastery long after Othmar's time. Happily, these poor beginnings gave the monks great zeal which their successors often lacked. Monk Vinithar relates how at that time his brethren, with no hesitation, had begged sheets of parchment to create their library. He himself would copy anything desired in exchange for a few of these precious sheets.

Walafrid Strabo also praises Othmar's charity and humility by relating several significant anecdotes. Often Othmar would return naked to the monastery after having given all his clothes to the poor.

One day, Pepin[29] gave him seventy silver marks; but he gave them away so generously to the poor as he traveled that he would have returned empty-handed had his companions not moderated his generosity. He created a shelter for lepers where he went by night to wash and dress their sores.

Though Othmar despised greatly the riches of this world, the same could not be said for Counts Warin and Ruadhart, whose rule was often naught but outrageous theft. Othmar complained of their conduct to Pepin who ordered them to restore all they had taken. They did no such thing, and when Othmar wished to report their behavior, they seized him and persuaded evil monks to accuse him of grave crimes. He was at first imprisoned in the Palace, and then sent to an island in the Rhine opposite Stein (Argovie). A harsh regime was imposed on him, and his evil jailers vexed him outrageously, treating him with such malice that he died on 16th November / 29th November 759.

Around 768 or 769, Othmar's body was brought back to Saint-Gall and laid to rest in the church. When it was rebuilt in 830, the relics were brought into the Church of St Peter in the cemetery next to the monastery. On 25th October / 7th November 864, they were brought back into the new Church of St Gall. Finally, on 24th September / 7th October 867, they were brought into the new Church of Saint Othmar in the presence of the monks of Reichenau and Kempten. From that time, the main feast of St Othmar has been celebrated with a vigil on 16th November / 29th November and the translation of his relics on 24th September / 7th October.

Saint Othmar, pray to God for us!

Troparion of Saint Othmar. Tone 4

Thou wast priest of the Church of Saint Firmin, / then abbot of Saint Gall. / Despising the vain riches of this world / and falsely accused, thou wast sent to die in exile. / Thy whole life was turned to the Lord. / Holy Father Othmar, pray to Christ our God to save our souls.

21ˢᵀ NOVEMBER / 4ᵀᴴ DECEMBER

The Life of Our Father among the Saints
Columbanus, Abbot of Luxeuil and Bobbio
(† 615 A.D.)
Feast day 21ˢᵗ November / 4ᵗʰ December

Saint Columbanus was born in Leinster, a kingdom of Ireland, in 543. When he was about twenty, he entered the famous Monastery of Bangor with its abbot, St Comgall, as his guide. He left the green shores of Ireland around 580 with St Gall and founded abbeys and communities all along his path between the Meuse and the Rhine as far as Germany. He left his disciples to preach the Gospel in these places which were still in the darkness of paganism.

He gave a most austere rule to these communities, "The Rule for Monks" (*Regula Monachorum*), the only rule of ancient Ireland to have

Fig 10 Fresco of Saint Columbanus on a column at Brugnato Cathedral in Italy.

survived to our day. With this he led many men to the borders of Paradise and holiness.

Among his disciples are St Faron of Meaux, St Babolin of Saint Maur des Fossés, St Donat of Besançon, St Omer of Thérouanne, St Romaric, St Wandrille, St Achaire, St Amand, St Philibert, St Valéry, and many more ascetics and preachers who adorn the pages of our Orthodox synaxaria.

Without doubt, the best known of his monasteries is Luxeuil in Franche-Comté, where monks came from different nations to seek salvation, including Franks, Gauls, and Burgundians. For two centuries it blossomed as the greatest monastic center in the West.

Saint Columbanus was a man of firm character, just, but strict with himself and with others whatever their social rank. He was obliged to leave Luxeuil in 610, chased away by Queen Brunehaut whose personal conduct, full of vice and crime, he had reproached.

He considered returning to Ireland and set off toward the place where he had arrived on the continent; however, obliged to turn back, he went first to Tuggen on Lake Zurich, then to Bregenz by Lake Constance to preach to the Alamans. Finally, he crossed the Alps and settled at Bobbio (Emilie-Romagne) where he founded his last monastery. In the year 615 he departed peacefully into heaven.

Saint Columbanus deserves to be numbered among the great army of the saints of Switzerland, for his coming brought great a fruitful blessing to the church of this land. He brought many to the Faith and after he had gone, his disciple St Gall (see his life on page 21) founded the greatest monastery of Switzerland.

Saint Columbanus, pray to God for us!

Troparion of Saint Columbanus of Luxeuil, Abbot. Tone 8

Thou camest from Ireland to furthest Gaul / and didst preach the Gospel to the pagan peoples. / Thou didst found a holy monastery at Luxeuil and Bobbio / whence thou didst depart to God. / Holy Father Columbanus, pearl amongst monks, / pray to the Lord that he may grant us His great mercy.

DECEMBER

2ᴺᴰ Dᴇᴄᴇᴍʙᴇʀ / 15ᵀᴴ Dᴇᴄᴇᴍʙᴇʀ

The Life of Our Father among the Saints

Lucius (Luce or Lutzi) of Coire

(Fifth or Sixth Century A.D.)
Feast day 2nd December / 15th December

Little is known of this saint apart from his martyrdom. Contrary to what was believed for many years, he was not the son of a British king who asked the Bishop of Rome to send Christian missionaries to England. In fact, he came from a region between Liechtenstein and Switzerland, and dwelt in a cave close to Coire. He preached to the pagans in that place but was falsely accused by the opponents of the Christian faith. He was then judged, condemned, and stoned to death near the Roman tower of Marsöl.

Fig 11 The Church of Saint Lucius with Saint Lucius Seminary, Coire (Chur).

39

It is said that his sister Emerita joined him there and was also martyred, but by fire (see her life below).

Saint Lucius, pray to God for us!

Troparion of Saint Lucius. Tone 5

Thy whole life was known only to the Lord. / Thou didst live in fasting and prayer far from the world and its vain troubles. / Dwelling in a cave thou didst preach the Gospel / before joining the ranks of the martyrs. / Saint Lucius, pray to Christ our God to save our souls.

4ᵗʰ December / 17ᵗʰ December

The Life of Our Mother among the Saints

Emerita

(Fifth or Sixth Century A.D.)
Feast day 4ᵗʰ December / 17ᵗʰ December

Tradition relates that Emerita lived in the fifth or sixth century. She was the sister of Lucius who was once thought to be the son of British king, but who most likely came from the north of the Grisons between Liechtenstein and Switzerland. She diligently visited the sick, comforting them and giving them generous alms. Later, she left her country with a few companions to visit her brother and to work with him for the glory of God.

Both came to Coire, where they dwelt in a cave and prepared for their future labors in Christ by prayer and fasting. Later, Emerita left Lucius to dwell in Trimmis and there preached the Gospel. But in this area, there dwelt cruel and hard-hearted pagans who caught her and whipped her. Then they cast her into prison before burning her alive as a martyr.

Saint Emerita, pray to God for us!

Troparion of Saint Emerita. Tone 8

Sister of the holy hermit Lucius, the martyr of Christ, / thou wast a perfect model of charity, / first with thy brother, then at Trimmis. / Then, after wandering through Italy, thou didst become a recluse in Switzerland. / Saint Emerita, pray to God to save our souls.

12ᵀᴴ December / 25ᵀᴴ December

The Life of Our Father among the Saints

Tranquillinus, Abbot of Agaunum

(† between 523 and 526 A.D.)
Feast day 12th December / 25th December

Tranquillinus was the successor to St Achive (see page 73) and is especially remembered as an abbot who was meek and calm as his name suggests. He is also remembered for his discovery of and care for the relics of King Sigismond and his martyred children found in the village well into which they were thrown after they had been killed.

Saint Tranquillinus, pray to God for us!

Troparion of Saint Tranquillinus. Tone 3

Successor to Saint Achive in the holy monastery / which sheltered the relics of the pious martyrs of the Theban Legion, / thou didst strive that Saint Sigismond / and all his children should be rightly honored in the Church. / Holy Father Tranquillinus, pray to Christ our God to save our souls.

16ᵀᴴ December / 29ᵀᴴ December

The Life of Our Father among the Saints
Ursannus, Disciple of Saint Columbanus
(✝ 619 A.D.)
Feast day 16ᵗʰ December / 29ᵗʰ December
and 20ᵗʰ December / 2ⁿᵈ January

Saint Ursannus was Irish and a disciple of St Columbanus. A monk of Luxeuil, he dwelt in the Swiss mountains and preached the Gospel to those who lived there. Tradition relates that he dwelt in a cave overlooking the Doubs with a bear as his companion. He worked many miracles and his fame attracted many of the faithful who were professed monks and who founded a monastery over his tomb. The place became the Swiss village of Saint-Ursanne. He is the patron saint of Soleure, Basel, and Porrentruy. He has feasts on 16ᵗʰ and 20ᵗʰ December / 29ᵗʰ December and 2ⁿᵈ January.

Troparion of Saint Ursannus, Abbot of Condat. Tone 1

Companion of the holy abbot Columbanus, / thou didst remain in Switzerland to preach the Gospel. / In the mountains of Jura thou didst live in prayer and fasting / as a perfect disciple. / And thy fame didst draw to thee many disciples. / Holy Father Ursannus, pray for our salvation to Christ our God.

31ˢᵀ December / 13ᵀᴴ January

Life of Our Father among the Saints
Marius, Bishop of Avenches and of Lausanne
(✝ 593 or 594 A.D.)
Feast day 31ˢᵗ December / 13ᵗʰ January

Marius came from a famous family and was born in 530 in the diocese of Autun. He was tonsured a monk, possibly in Saint-Symphorien of Autun, Avenches, or even Agaunum.

He was enthroned as Bishop of Avenches in 574 and took part in the Council of Macon in 585. Toward the end of his life, he transferred his see from Avenches to Lausanne where he died, being buried in the Church of Saint Thyrse where his relics were conserved. At the end of the sixth century, the church was rededicated to St Marius.

Tradition relates that as a bishop, Marius built in his diocese several churches dedicated to the martyrs of Autun. He is said to have brought the relics of these martyrs from his birthplace to his see. St Marius lived as a humble ascetic while fulfilling his episcopal duties. He also wrote a universal chronicle of events between 435 and 581.

Saint Marius, pray to God for us!

Troparion of Saint Marius. Tone 6

Born in Autun thou wast first tonsured a monk, / then consecrated bishop of the city of Avenches. / Thou didst transfer thy see to Lausanne / and in thy diocese didst build churches. / O admirable model of charity, / holy Father Marius, pray to Christ our God to save our souls.

JANUARY

The Life of Our Father among the Saints
Oyend (Eugendus)
(† 509 A.D.)
Feast day ¹ˢᵗ January / 14ᵗʰ January

Bishop Ambrose (Cantacuzène) of Vevey (1947–2009) mentions the holy Abbot of Condat, Oyend, in the litany of the Vigil in his parish, alongside Saints Romanus and Lupicinus, also great saints of the Jura. He also had him depicted in the icon of all the saints who have enlightened Switzerland. His abbey is situated close to the border of the diocese of Geneva.

Saint Oyend (Eugendus) was born around 450 near Izenore (or Izarnodurum, whose name in Celtic means "the iron gate," signifying the fortifications which enclosed it). He left for heaven in the peace of Christ in Condat, which later was called Saint-Oyend, then Saint-Claude. Oyend was a disciple of Saints Romanus and Lupicinus, and Abbot of the Monastery of Condat in the French Department of the Jura. He is celebrated on 1ˢᵗ January / 14ᵗʰ January.

His father was a priest who initiated him into the mysteries of God from his childhood and knew how to inspire in him love for the Church. When he was six years old, St Oyend told his father of a dream in which Saints Romanus and Lupicinus (who were then still alive and famed for their spiritual feats) came to raise him from his bed and place him at the doorway of the house with his face turned to the East. They showed him the stars, just as God had shown them to Abraham, and said: "Thus will be thy posterity." In the vision, he saw the two saints draw near to him with a vast crowd of monks. The heavens opened and the angels rose up and descended to the place where Oyend lay. They spoke many things, but all he heard was the word of the Lord: "I am the way, the truth and the life." (John 14:6).

His father decided that he should be educated in the Monastery of Condat. There, Saints Romanus and Lupicinus guided him in the spiritual life, and he hardly ever left the monastery until he was sixty years old. When Romanus died, he was succeeded by St Minasius, who became the new guide of this promising novice. Through his prayer and self-denial, Oyend was a model of monasticism. Minasius made him his helper and co-abbot. Although Minasius prayed and entreated Oyend so much, he could never persuade him to accept the priesthood, which the Holy Father refused through humility. According to one of his anonymous biographers (possibly Pragmatius[30]): "He took great pains to give each monk the obedience for which the Holy Spirit had best endowed him. As soon as he found free time, he readily took to reading the Holy Scriptures whether by day or by night."

Oyend had another vision of Romanus and Lupicinus who revealed that he was to replace Minasius after his departure from this life, and that trials awaited him. Shortly afterwards Minasius did indeed die, and in 496 Oyend was elected abbot. He continued to lead an austere life, always wearing the same tunic and the same hair shirt, eating only once a day. The predicted trials soon came: a group of monks, finding him too austere, left the monastery.

He ordered the life of the monastery according to the rule of Tarnade (the original name of the Monastery of Agaunum). The characteristic of this rule was the perpetual prayer (*laus perennis*) (which originated in the Monastery of Saint Marcel the Acemete in Constantinople. Moreover, he surrounded himself

Fig 12 Crypt of Saint Oyand (sixth century) and its colonnade (seventh century) at the Grenoble Archaeological museum.

with learned men to instruct all those called to the monastic life. They taught Holy Scripture, the Fathers, humanities, and the liberal arts (grammar, rhetoric, and music). They also taught practical woodwork and carving, and trained their pupils to copy manuscripts with great art and beauty. St Viventiole was one of these teachers who later became Bishop of Lyon and was glorified by the Church.

As predicted, further trials came. The holy place was burnt down. After the blaze, which reduced the monastery to ashes, Oyend rebuilt it completely. He replaced the small individual cells with a vast dormitory where he slept with his monks, and the original oratory became a church. He ate in the refectory with his monks, sharing the same food in their midst.

Oyend was well known for his miracles, especially for his prophecies of future events, but also for his cures of the sick and deliverance of the possessed. Through his prayers and his charity, he lightened the burden of the Christians who turned to him. He attached no importance to social rank but received every person as Christ Himself. His charity was such that there were often more visitors seeking his help than there were monks in the monastery.

In that age of war and conflict he prayed without ceasing for the peace of the world and for the conversion of the princes. He was never compromised by worldly power.

In 509 Oyend began to suffer from a sickness which would lead to his death. As was his habit, he stuck to his rule of one meal a day in spite of his weakness. His illness lasted for six months. He called to himself the monk Antidiole, the priest Pragmatius, and the other monks, and told them that he was about to depart to the heavenly homeland. Weeping, he revealed that Saints Romanus and Lupicinus had already come to take him, but that the prayers of his spiritual children, the monks, had kept him in the land of the living. He begged them to cease these prayers and to let him find the peace of Christ in heaven. Five days later, he appeared to fall asleep, but had already gone to join the holy fathers Romanus and Lupicinus.

Oyend was buried in Condat (now Saint-Claude) in the monastery which he had ruled and which was named after him until the thirteenth century. From the seventh century he was widely venerated as a saint. Saint Antidiole built a church where his relics were buried and later housing close by to receive the numerous pilgrims who came to ask for his intercession. The settlement grew eventually into town of Saint-Claude in the French Jura. Several churches are dedicated to him, and his name has been given to two towns: Saint-Oyen in Savoy and Saint-Oyen in the Val d'Aoste.

Saint Oyend, pray to God for us.

Troparion of Saint Oyend, Abbot of Condat. Tone 1

Companion of Saints Romanus and Lupicinus, / thou wast elected abbot though not a priest. / In the Jura, in the Abbey of Condat, /

God did grant thee the grace of healing. / Thou wast a most worthy father of monks; / holy Father Oyend, pray to God to have mercy on our souls.

7ᵀᴴ JANUARY / 20ᵀᴴ JANUARY

The Life of Our Father among the Saints
Valentinian, Bishop of Coire
(✝ 548 A.D.)
Feast day 7ᵗʰ January / 20ᵗʰ January

We know little of St Valentinian, who was Bishop of Coire. He developed the community founded by St Lucius, and founded a Benedictine monastery dedicated to this saint. He passed into heaven on 7ᵗʰ January /20ᵗʰ January 548 in Coire, and was buried in the crypt of the Church of Saint Lucius (Saint-Luzi).

Saint Valentinian, pray to God for us!

Troparion of Saint Valentinian, Bishop of Coire. Tone 1

Thou wast a holy hierarch in the town of Coire / and didst continue the work of Saint Lucius, / building up the community which he founded, / and by creating a Benedictine monastery thou didst glorify the Lord and His Church. / Holy Father Valentinian, / intercede for the salvation of our souls.

11ᵀᴴ JANUARY /24ᵀᴴ JANUARY

The Life of Our Father among the Saints
Ynnemod (or Hymnemode)
Abbot of Agaunum (Saint Maurice)
(† 516 A.D.)
Feast day 11ᵗʰ January / 24ᵗʰ January

Saint Ynnemod was one of the great abbots of the Monastery of Agaunum in the Valais. His date of birth is unknown. He was in the Monastery of Grigny close to Vienne in Dauphiné when the Bishops of the Council of Agaunum unanimously appointed him Abbot of Agaunum, a monastery richly endowed by King and Martyr Sigismond.

The martyrology of the monastery says this of him: "Ynnemod was a man of admirable patience, piety, and wisdom. The fathers of the Council of Agaunum, greatly admiring his holiness and meekness, entrusted him with the government of the Church of Agaunum. He gathered the nine hundred monks in the house of the Lord and gave them all a single rule. In all things he sought to please God in holiness, to grow therein more and more, and every day to progress in the study of salvation, soteriology."

Ynnemod organized the monks of the monastery into five choirs to chant the Psalter without ceasing: the perpetual prayer (*laus perennis*) which had been started by the pious King and Martyr Sigismond. This practice originated with St Marcel in the monastery of the "sleepless ones" (*acemetes*) in Constantinople. This perpetual praise took place day and night without interruption.

Just as St Marcel (†485) had an important role in the Council of Chalcedon, where the Monophysite heresy was condemned and the divine and human natures of Christ were defined, so St Ynnemod fought with tireless zeal against the Arian heresy which had grown and threatened the Orthodox in the Valais.

As he felt the end of his earthly life draw near, he called his monks to gather around him and exhorted them to live in love for one another according to the commandment of Christ. He passed into heaven on the 11ᵗʰ January / 18ᵗʰ January in the year 516. Though he was Abbot of the holy Monastery of Agaunum for only seven months, his pious work was often praised by his successors after his departure to heaven.

Saint Ynnemod, pray to God for us!

Troparion of Saint Ynnemod, Abbot of Agaunum. Tone 1

Thou wast a monk in the Monastery of Grigny / when the fame of thy great piety / caused thee to receive from Christ the office of abbot / of the holy Abbey of Agaunum. / Thou didst there preserve perpetual prayer / and thou didst fight the evil heresy of Arius. / Holy Father Ynnemod, pray to God to have mercy upon us.

21ˢᵗ January / 3ᴿᴰ February

The Life of Our Father among the Saints
Meinrad,
the Founder of *Notre Dame des Ermites* (Einsiedeln)
(† 861 A.D.)
Feast day 21ˢᵗ January / 3ʳᵈ February

Meinrad (Meinard, Meginard, Meinrard, Monhard, or Meginrad) was born into the family of the Counts of Hohenzollern. At baptism, he was given the name of Meginrad ("good council") which later became Meinrad. After spending ten to eleven years in his father's house, the young Meinrad went to study at the Benedictine Monastery of Reichenau on an island in Lake Constance. This island had been freed of reptiles, its only inhabitants at that time, by St Firmin and had become so pleasant and fertile under the care of the monks that its name had been changed to Reichenau (the rich plain). Two of his relatives, Hatto and Erlebald, had been abbots and there he was tonsured a monk.

Fig 13 Saint Meinrad

Reichenau was a seedbed for monks, bishops, and learned men, a fount of civilization and light.

Meinrad loved to read the works of spiritual masters. He especially liked St John Cassian and was fascinated by the lives of the Desert Fathers, and so dedicated himself to the Church of Christ. He was ordained deacon in 821, and then a priest. A learned connoisseur of the Fathers and of spiritual life through his pious reading, he set himself to practice what he had learned of the monastic tradition of the Church.

His deepest thought could be summed up in his saying to his pupils whom he was asked to teach at the Monastery of Bollengen: "Seek the truth with love, not to gain worldly glory, but simply for love of truth."

The love of God burnt within him and drove him to seek a closer link with God in solitude. In June 828, at the age of thirty-one, he withdrew to Mount Etzel, which was covered with thick dark forests. He took with him a commentary on the Gospels, the rule of St Benedict, and the works so dear to him of John Cassian.

At first, Meinrad lived sheltered by the branches of a tree and a rough wall built of stones which had broken from the mountain. Then a pious widow from Alterdorf had a hut and chapel built for him. He spent seven years there, but soon his peaceful retreat became a place of pilgrimage and people came from everywhere to seek his advice.

Behind Mount Etzel was a thick forest where he retired with another monk and a peasant from Bollengen. Finding a suitable place for his new dwelling, he settled there. On the way, he found a pine tree where there was a nest sheltering two crows who also became his companions.

The voice of the Gospel had never echoed in this savage place. Edwige, the Abbess of a small community of nuns in Zurich, cared for the needs of the pious hermit and replaced the widow of Alterdorf. Tradition relates that one day, at prayer, Meinrad was surrounded by a horde of demons, but an angel appeared and drove them off. From that day he redoubled his prayers and regained the grace that Adam had in Paradise: the wild beasts, eagles, and bears came to take their food from his hand, and the two crows perched on his shoulders. There he joined with the magnificent nature around him in praise of the Creator; for truly, in that Paradise of beauty and prayer as the Psalmist David said, "Let everything that hath breath praise the Lord" (Ps 150:6). Meinrad soon began to preach to the local people.

Crowds started once more to come to seek the holy father's advice. His fame spread far and wide. Hildegarde, whom her father Louis the German had appointed Abbess of the monastery in Zurich in 853, heard of the virtues of Meinrad. She came and built him a chapel, which remained standing until 1798. Meinrad consecrated it to the Holy Mother of God and Ever-Virgin Mary. He placed the statue of the Most Pure Mother of God which

Hildegarde had given him on the altar, and miracles abounded. Pilgrims who came to venerate the Mother of God received extraordinary grace, and the chapel was named the "Place of Grace." From the statue of the Virgin arose the pilgrimage of "Notre Dame d'Einsiedeln" (*Notre Dame des Ermites*).

The Bollandists relate how a cleric from Reichenau visited Meinrad. One night, he saw the small chapel illuminated by a flash of light. He went in, and saw St Meinrad kneeling on the altar steps while an angel stood beside him holding a prayer book and joining his voice to the saint's.

Two men were tempted by a demon: Peter from Grisors and Richard the Swabian. They decided to murder the saint and steal his treasures, believing them to be immense since they thought he must have received many gifts from his numerous visitors. Not far from the Lake of Zurich was the Inn of Endigen, later to become Rappeswil, and there they spent the night. At first light they set out for the Etzel and headed toward the forest. It was 21st January / 3rd February 861. Since snow had covered all the paths, they lost their way and wandered for some time through the woods. However, the devil directed their steps toward the hermitage of St Meinrad. As they drew near, the two crows shrieked loudly and flew round and round the hut in their alarm, greatly surprising the two murderers.

They arrived at the door of the chapel as the sun rose. As was his custom, the saint had prayed at length. He had celebrated the office before the image of the Mother of God and taken communion of the Holy Mysteries of Christ. The brigands knocked on the door. As though he had been warned by heaven of what was to come, Meinrad prayed intensely once more then came to open the door to them. He received them cordially and said: "My friends if you had come earlier, you might have taken part in the Office. Come in and pray to God and the Saints to bless you. Come into my cell. I will share with you the scant provisions which remain to me. Then you will accomplish the work for which you came here."

The murderers went into the chapel for a few minutes, but fearing that their victim might escape, they rushed into the cell and cruelly put him to death. Their evil deed done, the two murderers fled pursued by the crows of the holy father Meinrad who had gone to join his beloved Master.

Chased by the crows, the two murderers were arrested. The Abbot of Reichenau sent two monks to bring the body of the saint to the Monastery of Ill, but they could not move the blessed remains of the martyr. They placed the heart of the saint in the chapel and then took his relics to Reichenau where a chapel was built in his honor.

Since the time of his martyrdom St Meinrad has continued his mission on earth from heaven where he now dwells. The miracles from his intercession have never ceased. Even today, the pilgrimage to *Notre Dame des Ermites* attracts the pious to the shrine of the Most Pure Mother of God.

Holy martyr Meinrad, pray to God for us!

Troparion of Saint Meinrad, Martyr. Tone 8

Thou wast the sprout of an illustrious family. / Thou didst leave the world to go toward God. / Thou didst seek the peace of God in self-denial, / and didst found the Monastery of Einsiedeln. / As a martyr thou didst find the Kingdom. / Holy martyr Meinrad, intercede for our souls.

31ST JANUARY / 13TH FEBRUARY

The Life of Our Father among the Saints
Eusebius, Monk of the Monastery of Saint Gall, then Hermit
(† 884 A.D.)
Feast day 31st January / 13th February

Saint Eusebius came from Ireland and was professed a monk at the Monastery of Saint Gall. Attracted to the solitary life, he was blessed to live in the hermitage of Mount Saint-Victor (Viktorsberg), close to Rankweil in the Voralberg.

He was murdered by those who dwelt there for his condemnation of their vices. They cut off his head with the blade of a scythe on 31st January / 13th February 884. Saint Eusebius, pray to God for us!

Troparion of Saint Eusebius of Saint Gall, Martyr. Tone 5

Coming from Ireland to preach the Gospel, / thou wast professed a monk in the Monastery of Saint Gall, / then didst leave to be a hermit on Mount Saint Victor. / There thou didst rebuke the vice of those who dwelt there, / but far from repenting they didst slay thee as a martyr. / Saint Eusebius, pray to God to have mercy upon us.

FEBRUARY

1ˢᵗ February / 14ᵀᴴ February

The Life of Our Father among the Saints
Faustus of Agaunum
(✝ 513 A.D.)
Feast day 1ˢᵗ February / 14ᵗʰ February

Faustus entered the Monastery of Agaunum around 470 A.D. He wrote the first life of St Severin (see page 60), his father in Christ and recounted the various miraculous events which took place during St Severin's voyage through France. After the death of his father in Christ, he returned from these travels and most likely succeeded him as Abbot of Agaunum.

It was St Faustus who was elected to replace Abbot Severin with whom he had shared the spiritual life for thirty-two years since he was the best prepared to continue the noble way of his role model and revered master. He followed him as far as his departure to heaven, and when God took St Severin from this life, Faustus, who so revered him, not only wrote his life, but imitated him ever more closely, showing forth the same virtues and gaining the same fame of piety. Faustus received the same gift of miracles as his spiritual father and departed to heaven on 1ˢᵗ February / 14ᵗʰ February 513. He fell asleep peacefully in Christ at Château-Landon which he happened to be visiting.

Saint Faustus, pray to God for us!

Troparion of Saint Faustus, Abbot of Agaunum. Tone 7

Thou wast a worthy disciple of Saint Severin / whose path thou didst follow in the land of France. / Thou didst write of his life and miracles and didst return to the holy Monastery of Agaunum / to take up the work of abbot that had been his. / Holy Father Faustus, pray to the Lord to save our souls.

11ᵀᴴ FEBRUARY / 24ᵀᴴ FEBRUARY

The Life of Our Father among the Saints
Severin, Abbot of the Monastery of Saint Maurice in Agaunum
(†507 A.D.)
Feast day 1ˢᵗ February / 14ᵗʰ February

Three accounts of the life of this holy father of Switzerland have come down to us: the life by Sirius, the life published by the Bollandists,[31] and the life written by St Faustus (see above) who for thirty years was the companion and disciple of the saint. This last life, the primitive one, is the most authentic, while the others simply re-work it with various additions.

Saint Severin was born in 440 A.D. to an illustrious family in Burgundy. At that time, the Arian heresy[32] was widely followed, but the saint had the good fortune to grow up and be educated in a family which practiced the Orthodox Faith.

Through his birth he might have gained a high position in the society of his day, but preferred to abandon the illusions of this world. At an early age, he entered the Monastery of Agaunum (now Saint-Maurice).

In those days the monastery consisted of a modest chapel, built against a rocky cliff with some guest rooms for pilgrims and a small cloister for the monks who guarded the precious relics of the saints of the glorious Theban Legion.

Fig 14 King Clovis is miraculously cured through the prayers of St Severin, and in gratitude, the king offers him money to distribute to the poor.

His companion, Faustus, tells us that Severin was a monk above reproach. He was inspired with great piety and dwelt constantly in God through his love and great humility. In 476, when the Abbot of Agaunum departed to the heavenly realm, Severin was the natural choice to succeed him as head of the community.

Severin was a father who loved his monks, a light for those gone astray, and a solace for the sick and suffering. All sought his prayer as they sought the Source of Life. His great fervor and humility brought him the gift of miracle working from God. He used it generously for the benefit of those around him, assuaging the pain of men.

His reputation grew and spread beyond the frontiers. It came to pass that Clovis, King of the Franks,[33] was struck down by a dangerous fever. They feared for his life, and none of the remedies known to human medicine could help him. Even his doctor suggested that he summon to his bedside a holy man of whom men spoke with great veneration. Clovis at once sent one of his servants to Agaunum to the holy abbot.

A little while earlier, Severin had seen the vision of an angel who revealed that he would soon depart to a far country where he would surrender his soul to God and be buried. Resolved to go to the king who had called him and understanding that this vision announced his blessed departure to heaven, the abbot gathered his monks and bade them farewell. Then he left.

His path was sown with miracles. In Nevers, he visited the cathedral in prayer and asked to see the bishop. The bishop was sick, but when the saint arrived, he was straightway healed. Then he continued his journey in prayer. Entering Paris he met a leper and anointed him with saliva, healing him at once. He comforted many other suffering people through his prayers, bringing the healing of their distress in the name of God.

When Severin came into the presence of King Clovis, he knelt down and prayed. He took off his cloak and spread it out over the king who was instantly freed from his fever. The grateful king gave him precious gifts, freeing prisoners from the jails. The saint worked further miracles before starting out on his journey home.

He left Paris and went toward Château-Landon en Gâtinais (now in the Department of Seine-et-Marne). On a hill stood an oratory[34] served by two priests, Ursicin and Paschase. He revealed to them his vision and his coming departure to the heavenly realm. and confided to their care his companions Faustus and Vital.

Abiding in God through prayer during his last days in the land of the living, St Severin was ready to join to his Father in heaven on 11ᵗʰ February / 24ᵗʰ February 507. A great light shone forth as he left for the heavenly realm.

Childebert,[35] the son of King Clovis, had a church built over the tomb of the saint where many miracles had witnessed to the favor of the Lord for Abbot Severin. A community was organized around his relics, and St Faustus left to tell the monks of Agaunum of the repose of St Severin. There, it believed that he was elected abbot. He then left on a pilgrimage to return to the tomb of his spiritual father. A church was also constructed in his name in Paris, which exists to this day.

The previously mentioned church in Château-Landon which sheltered his relics was twice destroyed: once by the Saxons and then by the English. Fortunately, the relics were saved on both occasions. In 1568, the Calvinists occupied the monastery and pillaged its treasures. They took a silver reliquary of an arm, threw away the relic and kept the silver. The arm of the saint, thus discarded, shone with an extraordinary light which was seen by the local peasants. They told the priest of the neighboring parish who took the precious relic to a safe place.

The French Revolution destroyed the last relics of St Severin in France. The feast of the saint was fixed on 11ᵗʰ February / 14ᵗʰ February on the anniversary of his departure to heaven. One of his relics has been preserved in Saint-Maurice in the Valais.

Saint Severin, pray to God for us!

Troparion of Saint Severin, Abbot of Agaunum. Tone 2

Monk of the holy Monastery of Saint Maurice, / for thy pious life thou wast elected abbot. / Miracle worker of great renown, / thou didst go to heal Clovis the King of the Franks / and didst depart to heaven on the road of return./ Holy Father Severin, pray to God to save our souls.

21ˢᵗ FEBRUARY / 5ᵀᴴ MARCH

The Life of Our Fathers among the Saints
Germain and Randoald, Martyrs
(+666 A.D.)
Feast day 21ˢᵗ February / 5ᵗʰ March

Germain was the son of a wealthy senator from Trier. After the death of his parents, he was educated by Modoald, the Bishop of Trier, who was present at the Council of Reims in 624. When he was seventeen years old, he sold all his goods and gave his wealth to the poor. At first, he entered the Monastery of Saint Romaric, whose abbot was St Arnulphe of Metz. Later, he traveled to the Monastery of Luxeuil, founded by St Columbanus, where he was tonsured a monk under Abbot Waldebert. The chronicle of his life relates: "Submitting his whole body to fasting, vigil, and prayer, he strove towards God receiving nothing but his daily provisions. His clothing was of the plainest, and he gave an example of humility and charity to all. When he would cut wood in the forest with his companion, he carried it all home on his back. He meditated on the saying of the blessed Paul:

'If anyone will not work, neither shall he eat.' [2 Thess 3:10]."[36]

He grew spiritually in self-denial and prayer to the wonder of his brothers. Duke Gondoin, one of the leading nobles of Alsace, wished to found a monastery at Grandval in the diocese of Basel. He appealed to the Abbot of Luxeuil and his monks. Germain was chosen to become the first abbot of Moutier-Grandval whither he departed with Randoald and a few other monks. They built roads, and by devoting themselves to the poor lived a God-pleasing life.

After several peaceful years Cathic,[37] the Duke of Alsace and father of the future St Odile (a cruel and unstable man) devastated the whole valley of Delemont and the surrounding countryside. Germain and Randoald,[38] the prior, went to meet him in their priestly vestments. They met him by the Church of Saint Maurice in Courtelle where they bravely rebuked his outrageous behavior and urged him to spare the poor and innocent objects of his spite.

He promised to do so, and they returned to pray in the church of the holy martyr Maurice: however, his soldiers continued to pillage.

When the holy monks had finished their prayers, they set out on the road to Grandval. One of Cathic's men, with several accomplices, pursued them. They caught them and slew them with lances on 21st February / 5th March 666.

The martyrdom of the saints was recorded soberly by the hagiographer, the priest Bobolenus only a few years after their death.

Miracles took place at the tomb of St Germain and at the place of the two saints' martyrdom. The year after his departure to heaven, on Christmas Eve, "a great and brilliant light descended from heaven to the place where lay the mutilated body of the blessed one and filled all who saw it with wonder and great fear."[39]

Holy martyrs Germain and Randoald, pray to God for us!

Troparion of Saints Germain and Randoald, Martyrs. Tone 5

Both of you were monks sent from Luxeuil to Grandval. / Ye grew in prayer and fasting. / Ye didst worthily rebuke a tyrant / who oppressed your spiritual sheep by sowing death. / Ye were martyred through treachery. / Holy Fathers Germain and Randoald, pray to God for us.

28TH FEBRUARY / 12TH MARCH

The Life of Our Fathers among the Saints
Romanus (Feast day 28th February / 12th March) and
Lupicinus of Condat (Feast day 21st March / 3rd April),
and of Their Sister, Saint Yole (Feast day Unknown)
(Fifth Century)

Saints Romanus and Lipicinus were two brothers who were born around the end of the fourth century at Izenore (now in the Department of Ain in France). Romanus was endowed with the great virtues of charity and virginity. He refused to marry and placed himself in obedience to Abbot Sabin of the Monastery of Ainay in Lyon. He took Romanus into his care and initiated him into monastic life.

Around the age of thirty-five St Romanus left for the forests of the Jura and settled in Condat where he built a small hermitage. There he spent his time in prayer and manual work, living in self-denial among the wild beasts.

Lupicinus, meanwhile, lost his fiancée. After his father departed to heaven, he decided to join his brother Romanus in his prayerful solitude. Their life in the desert was harsh, for they were attacked many times by the demons and were finally obliged to abandon the hermitage. They spoke of their trials to a compassionate woman who took them and calmed them down. After they regained their strength and courage, they settled at the bottom of a gorge beneath a great pine tree. In this place the Monastery of Condat slowly developed as new disciples soon arrived to form a community governed by the two brothers.

Romanus was meek and guided the monks as a father, whereas Lupicinus was strict and his decisions were often quite hard to bear, although they were softened by the charity of Romanus. Lupicinus slept on a bench and ate only once every three days. He never drank wine, and for the last eight years of his life he drank nothing, not even water. According to tradition it was enough for him to put his hands in water for his thirst to be quenched.

As the number of their disciples grew, Lupicinus took some of them to found a new monastery at Lauconne. Both monasteries were always under the authority of both brothers, brothers according to the flesh and perfect brothers in Christ.

In the year 444, Celidoine, Bishop of Besançon, [40] was deposed since he had married a widow before ordination. Saint Hilarion of Arles[41] came to Besançon for this purpose and to reestablish discipline. There he heard the praises of St Romanus and heard of his virtues. He sent for him and ordained him to the priesthood.

Romanus became so famous for these virtues which had led him to the priesthood that he was obliged to build new monasteries in the Vosges, and even in Germany. Among them was one in the Vaud, later called Romain-Moutier and then Romainmôtier (the Monastery of Romanus).

Once, according to tradition, Romanus made a pilgrimage to the tomb of St Maurice at Agaunum and was caught in a sudden thunderstorm. He sheltered in a hut for lepers where he spent the night with no fear of the dreaded sickness of his hosts and the risk of infection. At dawn, he left for Agaunum. When the lepers awoke, they saw that they were completely healed: all their leprosy had disappeared. In their gratitude they ran after St Romanus to thank him but they could not catch him. Afterwards they spread abroad the marvelous news of this miracle.

Romanus wrote a monastic rule based on the practice of the monks of Lerins. He is the one who introduced the ban on meat for monks.

His sister, Yole, came to join him and founded a women's monastery at La Balme close to Lauconne. This is all we know of the life of this pious woman who followed her brothers on the monastic path. It was in this monastery that St Romanus desired to rest in Christ, and his body was taken there after his blessed dormition in 460 (or 473). This monastery, where his relics were kept, was thereafter named Saint-Romain-de-la-Roche.

Lupicinus survived him and continued to rule the monasteries he had founded with him. He died circa 480 (or 493).

Saints Romanus, Lupicinus, and Yole, pray to God for us!

Troparion of Saint Romanus of the Jura. Tone 1

As an admirer of the ancient Desert Fathers with thy beloved brother Lupicinus / thou didst found in the mountains of Jura the most famous Monastery of Condat, / and close by, the Monastery of Lauconne. / Holy Father Romanus, pray to Christ our God to have mercy upon us.

Troparion of Saint Lupicinus of the Jura. Tone 2

Brother of Saint Romanus in the flesh and in faith, / with thy beloved brother thou didst settle as a hermit in the mountains of Jura. / With him thou didst found two holy monasteries, / the sacred havens of Condat and Lauconne. / Holy Father Lupicinus, pray to God to have mercy upon us.

Troparion of Saint Yole. Tone 3

Sister of the holy brothers Romanus and Lupicinus, / thou didst join them in Christ as a nun. / Thou didst found a convent at La Balme, / and the rest of thy life was hidden in God / as thou dwelt under the gaze of our Lord. / Holy Mother Yole, pray the Lord our God to save us.

MARCH

21ST MARCH / 3RD APRIL

The Life of Our Father among the Saints
Lupicinus of Condat
(† 480 or 493 A.D.)
Feast day 21st March / 3rd April

(See his life on page 66 with his brother Saint Romanus 28th February / 12th March)

Troparion of Saint Lupicinus of the Jura. Tone 2

Brother of Saint Romanus in the flesh and in faith, / with thy beloved brother thou didst settle as a hermit in the mountains of Jura. / With him thou didst found two holy monasteries, / the sacred havens of Condat and Lauconne. / Holy Father Lupicinus, pray to God to have mercy upon us.

Fig 15 Saint Lupicinus a "desert dweller" of the Jura mountains founded an abbey at Lauconne, in the present day city of Saint-Lupicin, where he was buried. This is the church of St Lupicin in the monastery of Lauconne.

28ᵀᴴ MARCH / 10ᵀᴴ APRIL

The Life of Our Father among the Saints

Tutilon, Monk of Saint-Gall

(✝ 898 A.D.)

Feast day 28th March / 10th April

Tutilon was an exemplary monk of Saint-Gall, a poet, musician, painter, and sculptor. His friends in the world greatly admired his talents and regretted that he was enclosed in a monastery; however, our father Tutilon had chosen the better part of which the Gospel speaks. He continued with prayer piously to fulfill his monastic obedience until he departed peacefully to Christ on 28th March / 10th April 898.

Saint Tutilon, pray to God for us!

Troparion of Saint Tutilon. Tone 5

Man of many talents, thou didst leave the world, / to follow the narrow way of the Gospel. / Thou wast tonsured a monk in the Monastery of Saint Gall, / offering thy many talents to the Master of souls, / before departing to Him in His holy Kingdom. / Saint Tutilon, pray to Christ our God to save our souls.

29ᵀᴴ MARCH / 11ᵀᴴ APRIL

The Life of Our Father among the Saints
Achive, Third Abbot of Agaunum (Saint Maurice)
(† circa 520 to 523 A.D.)
Feast day 29th March / 11th April

When Ynnemod (or Hymnemode, †516), the Abbot of Grigny (near Vienna in Gaul) left, he wished that the monk Achive should be his successor. However, he refused and followed his master to Agaunum where he was happy living as a monk. When Abbot Ambrose died, he was elected to replace him. Achive was a great man of prayer, ascetic and strict. Tradition relates that his face "shone like the sun" when he was at prayer.

Saint Achive, pray to God for us!

Troparion of Saint Achive, Abbot of Agaunum (Saint Maurice). Tone 6

Ynnemod wished thee to be his successor / as Abbot of the holy Monastery of Agaunum; / but refusing this honor thou didst remain a monk / until elected abbot on the death of Ambrose. / Thou didst become as a spiritual sun. / Holy Father Achive, pray to Christ our God to save our souls.

APRIL

6ᵀᴴ April / 19ᵀᴴ April

The Life of Our Father among the Saints
Notker the Stammerer,
Monk of the Monastery of Saint Gall
(† 912 A.D.)
Feast day 6ᵗʰ April / 19ᵗʰ April

Saint Notker bore the Latin nickname *Balbulus* ("the Stammerer") because he stuttered. He was born around the middle of the ninth century at Heiligenau in Thurgovia to a distinguished family. He was educated in the Monastery of Saint Gall and was tonsured a monk when he reached adulthood.

He made great progress in music, for which he had a calling. There were two schools of music in Saint-Gall: one was in the monastery, and the other outside the precincts. Saint Notker became director of the former.

When he had time, he composed various musical works and copied manuscripts. Soon, his talents and his holiness became so renowned that even the Emperor, Charles the Fat,[42] would take his advice on difficult questions which arose in his realm. One day, he sent an officer to ask his advice on an important matter. Notker happened to be in the garden, uprooting weeds which he replaced with good plants. The messenger told him of his matter and Notker

Fig 16 St Notker the Stammerer

simply replied: "You see what I am doing. Tell the Emperor to do the same."

One day, the emperor came to Saint-Gall in person to consult the pious monk whom he saw as his friend and spiritual counselor. The emperor's chaplain was a learned man, but full of pride. His jealousy was aroused at the sight of his master placing all his trust in this monk who seemed so simple and ignorant. He said to himself as the humble Notker drew nigh: "I'll ask him a question which will show up his ignorance. Tell me my learned friend, what is God doing now in heaven?"

"He is raising up the humble and putting down the proud," replied the humble monk in all simplicity. The chaplain was outraged at such speech which put him to shame. He left the monastery at once. However, his horse reared up and he fell, wounding his face and breaking a leg. The monks rushed to help him and took him back into the monastery to care for him.

But their care did not prevent his state from worsening, so he was advised to ask for the pious prayers of Notker. Filled with immense pride and bitterness at Notker for his reply to the impious question he had posed, he refused. Yet the sickness progressed, and the pain grew ever stronger. At last he yielded to reason. "Bring to me the servant of God so that he may forgive me and bless me, unworthy as I am." Notker came to him and prayed fervently; and the chaplain felt immediate relief.

Notker departed to heaven on 6th April / 19th April 912 and his body was buried in the Chapel of Saint Peter. Several miracles took place at his tomb, so he was celebrated as a saint at Saint-Gall with his feast on the third Sunday after Easter.

The blessed Notker is the author of a martyrology based in part on those of Adon[43] and Raban Maur.[44] For many years it was used in most of the churches of Germany.

The holy monk Notker has also left us other works: there is a treatise on the interpreters of Holy Scripture in which he indicates which fathers have given the best commentaries on different aspects of the books of the Bible. He also provides a list from the "Acts of the Martyrs" (*Acta Martyrum*) which he considers sincere and authentic.

He produced a collection of thirty-eight sequences. These compositions shortened the canticles (which had formerly been very long) of the Church and made them more precise. He does not claim to have written these sequences, but states that they are created on the model of those found in the antiphonary of the Abbey of Jumieges in Neustria (Normandy).

He wrote the following sequence, translated from the Latin to the French and then to the English. It filled the faithful with joy during the Paschal feasts:

To the Paschal Victim the Christians offer a sacrifice of praise.
The Lamb has ransomed the sheep.
Christ, the innocent, has reconciled sinners to their Father.
Death and Life have met in a wonderous duel.
The Guide of Life, though dead, living reigneth.
Tell us, Mary, what didst thou see on the path?
I saw the tomb of the Living Christ
And the glory of His Resurrection,
The angelic witnesses, the shroud, and His clothes.
Christ, our hope, is risen.
He has gone before His disciples to Galilee.
We know that Christ is truly risen from the dead,
Do Thou, O conquering King, have mercy upon us. Amen

Also attributed to him is the following hymn which medieval Christian armies would sing before going into battle. It has an unusual origin. Saint Notker was struck by the great danger in which some workmen labored as they built a bridge over a deep gorge. He wrote this beautiful prayer for them.

Though living we are always threatened by death.
Who will help us if not Thou O Lord,
Thou Who art rightly vexed with us
Because of our sins?
Our fathers hoped in Thee, O Holy God
And Thou didst deliver them,
Thou didst deliver them.
Our fathers prayed to Thee, they prayed to Thee
And they were not confounded.
Holy God and Strong!
When our hair is whitened with age
And the years have broken our strength
Abandon us not.
Holy God and Merciful
Leave us not in the pains of death.

Saint Notker also wrote various hymns. Four are in honor of St Stephen the martyr, patron of the Cathedral of Metz. They were dedicated to Ruobert, the Bishop of Metz (†917), who had once been a monk of Saint-Gall.

He wrote on music, and what remains is in *The Latin Patrology* (*Patrologia Latina*),[45] LXXXI col §69. 1178.

The saint also wrote a life of St Gall in verse, and a treatise on the fractions of numbers. Only a fragment remains, but it shows his interest in mathematics.

A psalter in Old High German, which is sometimes attributed to him, was most probably written by another Notker (Labeo or the German, † 1012).

Saint Notker, pray to God for us!

Troparion of Saint Notker the Stammerer, Monk of the Monastery of Saint Gall. Tone 2

Pious monk of the sacred Monastery of Saint Gall, / thou didst lead a Christian life of virtue, / immersed in prayer, abstinence, and song. / For thou didst enrich the Church with music / and with the prayers that thou didst compose for Her. / Holy Father Notker, pray to God that He may save our souls.

MAY

1ˢᵗ May / 14ᵗʰ May

The Life of Our Father among the Saints
Sigismond, King of Burgundy
(† 524 A.D.)
Feast day 1ˢᵗ May / 14ᵗʰ May

Saint Sigismond was the son of Gondebaud, the Arian King of Burgundy. Through the influence of St Avit of Vienne (feast day 5ᵗʰ February / 18ᵗʰ February) he was converted to Orthodoxy. When he ascended the throne of Burgundy in 516, Sigismond showed great care for the life of the Orthodox Church.

He had been made co-ruler by his father from 513 and was crowned in Geneva. At that time, he was named Patrician of the Empire in Gaul, a dignity which was granted by the Eastern Emperors to the Burgundian princes who took great pride in these titles.

Sigismond called councils against the Arians and restored the Monastery of Agaunum. In fact, he founded the Monastery itself, for previously it had simply been a place where holy hermits lived in separate cells.

In 517 his zeal led him to summon the Council of Epaone which was presided by St Avit. He tried thus to purge his kingdom of the poisons of vice and heresy.

Despite his piety, Sigismond was still a man of his time: an impulsive barbarian with certain crude habits. After the death of his first wife, Ostrogotha, the daughter of the king of Italy, he remarried. But there was fierce hostility between his son, Sigeric, and his new wife. One day at a feast, the son reproached his stepmother for wearing the garments of his late mother. She was filled with rage and started, with insidious words, to incite Sigismond to murder his son, suggesting that Sigeric wished to kill his father and seize the kingdom for himself.

Fig 17 Saint Sigismund

Convinced by this slanderous accusation of plotting, the king fell into his wife's trap. Driven by the devil, he had his son strangled in his presence. Yet as soon as the crime was accomplished, he broke into tears and fell upon the dead body of his son. He went straight to Agaunum (now the Monastery of Saint-Maurice in the Valais) to try to atone for his sin with strict penitence. Tradition relates that an elder told him: "It is for yourself that you should weep now, for by following treacherous advice you have become a cruel murderer. He whom you caused to die in innocence has no need of tears!"

The king passed many long days in tears and fasting, begging God for forgiveness. He prayed God to send him his punishment here in this earthly life. It was during this stay in the Monastery of Agaunum that he decreed the *perpetual prayer* (*laus perennis*) inspired by the tradition of the Acemetes of Saint Marcel in Constantinople. Taking advantage of the weakness of the Kingdom of Burgundy, the Frankish princes of the North declared war on him. Defeated, King Sigismond fled to a place then called Verrosa (now Verrosaz) where he lived as a hermit in a cave which remains to this day.

Fig 18 Place of King Sigismund's martyrdom. His body was thrown into this well by his executioners and a church was built around it. Water from this well is known to cure sicknesses.

His hair was shorn. and he wore the habit of a monk. A few Burgundians came to join him and advised him to settle in the Monastery of Agaunum, but this was a trap. On his way to the monastery, he was captured and taken to Gaul. There he was thrown into a well with his wife and children who were already the prisoners of Clodomir, one of his fiercest enemies.

God heard the prayer of His servant and allowed his crime to be punished by the revolt of his subjects. But He glorified his repentance by granting miracles at his tomb. Like the penitent King and Prophet David, he was glorified as a saint.

The body of the saint lay for three years in the well. Oftentimes, a lamp was seen miraculously lighting the place. People flocked to venerate the holy king. Little by little, they built a chapel surrounded by houses creating a village which was called Saint-Sigismond's-Well. but has now been shortened to Saint-Sigismond.[46]

However, it was at Agaunum that the saint became famous. His relics were transferred there, to a place now called Saint-Maurice in the Valais. Part of them (his head) was transferred to Prague. He was venerated as a martyr and miracles took place over his relics.

Saint Gregory of Tours, who died seventy-one years after the death of St Sigismond in 595, related in his book of martyrs and confessors how the faithful in his day were cured of fevers through the intercession of the saint. He was also famous for curing hernias.

An ancient prayer, included in the works of Saint Gregory of Tours, bears witness to the power of the saint's intercession for the pious faithful afflicted with fever:

"It is as a pure gift, O Lord, that in the name of Thy chosen one, Sigismond, and by the communion of the Body and Blood of Jesus Christ Thy Son, that Thou wilt drive away from Thy servant [N.] . . . here before Thee the shivering and heat of fever, and that Thou wilt grant him his former health. Amen!"

Troparion of Saint Sigismond, King of Burgundy and Martyr. Tone 4

O holy King and Martyr Sigismond, / by thine example thou dost guide us on the path of repentance. / By showing us the mercy of Christ / thou openest for us the doors of Paradise, / and thou bringest us to the loving arms of the Father. / Pray to the Lord of compassion that he may grant salvation to our souls.

Kontakion. Tone 2

Like the Holy King and Prophet David, / thou didst stain thy soul by a shameful murder. / But having lost the grace of our God, / in fasting and repentance thou didst seek once more the path to the

Heavenly Kingdom. / Thy sacrifice to the merciful Christ / joined thee once more to the Love of God. / Pray to Him for us sinners that He may grant us His mercy and salvation to our souls.

1ˢᵗ MAY / 14ᵀᴴ MAY

The Life of Our Mother among the Saints

Wiborade, Virgin and Martyr

(✝ 926 A.D.)

Feast day 1ˢᵗ May / 14ᵗʰ May

Saint Wiborade was from a noble family in Thurgovia. Her name is derived from Weiberat, which means "counselor of women." When she was still young, she was greatly affected by the premature death of her sister which led her to abandon the illusions of this world and to devote herself to a life of self-denial and charity.

After the death of her father, she took care of her sick and aged mother. She was close to her brother, Hitto, who was then a student at the Monastery of Saint Gall, where he was later tonsured a monk. Together, they worked out their salvation in Christ. She wove cloth for binding the books in the library. The library was later preserved during the Hungarian invasion and as a result, she became the patron of librarians.

When on a pilgrimage to Rome with her brother, she decided to withdraw as a hermit at Constance, and later to a cell in Saint George's Church. In 916, she became a recluse, confined by Bishop Solomon III close to the Church of Saint Magnus. Other women followed her example and formed a community of anchorites in the shadow of the Monastery of Saint Gall. Through a small window in her cell, Wiborade counseled clergy, nobles, and people of Saint-Gall.

Several prophecies are attributed to her of which the most famous is her prediction of the Hungarian invasion. She persuaded the Abbot of Saint-Gall to hide the library and the treasure of the church securely, but for her part she resolved to stay in her cell.

On 1ˢᵗ May / 14ᵗʰ May 926, Wiborade, who had not fled but remained so as to keep her vow of stability, was slain by three blows from an axe wielded by the barbarian invaders.

She is celebrated on 1ˢᵗ May / 14ᵗʰ May, the anniversary of her departure into heaven. In the West, she was celebrated on 2ⁿᵈ May / 15ᵗʰ May since another important saint was already commemorated on that day.

Saint Wiborade, pray to God for us!

Troparion of Saint Wiborade. Tone 2

As a pious nun and recluse close to Saint Gall / thou did lead a virtuous Christian life. / Given to self-denial thou didst not shrink from the trial, /and did not flee from a martyr's death, / but went to meet thy Heavenly Bridegroom Christ. / Saint Wiborade, pray to God to save our souls.

7ᵀᴴ MAY / 20ᵀᴴ MAY

The Life of Our Father among the Saints
Gaudence, Shepherd and Martyr
(† Fourth Century)
Feast day 7ᵗʰ May /20ᵗʰ May

Gaudence herded sheep in the Grisors until he became a shepherd of the flock of Christ by preaching the Gospel in the Bergell to the pagans of that place. He opposed a tyrannical man who was mistreating his spiritual flock and was martyred, slain by the stroke of a sword on the Feast of the Ascension, 7ᵗʰ May/ 20ᵗʰ May that year.

A church was built near Casaccia to shelter his relics and remained a much-frequented place of pilgrimage until the sixteenth century.

Saint Gaudence, pray to God for us!

Troparion of Saint Gaudence, Shepherd and Martyr. Tone 3

Thou didst herd thy sheep in the Grisors / and then became a shepherd of the Kingdom. / Thou didst preach the Gospel to the heathen, / and didst die a martyr on the day of the Ascension, / giving thy life for thy spiritual flock. / Holy Father Gaudence, pray to God that He may save our souls.

9ᵀᴴ May / 22ᴺᴰ May

The Life of Our Father among the Saints
Achates, the Companion of Saint Beatus

(† 118 A.D.)
Feast day 9th May / 22nd May

Achates, or Achatus, was the companion of St Beatus. Little is known of his life save that he lived as a hermit with St Beatus in a cave, now called Beatenberg, by the lake of Thoune.

Saint Achates, pray to God for us!

Troparion of the Hermits Saint Achates and Saint Beatus. Tone 4

Becoming hermits for the glory of God, / ye dwelt in self-denial and prayer. / In the spirit ye stood at the edge of heaven, / and after such lives devoted to Him, / ye were taken by Christ into His Kingdom. / Saints Beatus and Achates, pray to God for us.

9ᵀᴴ MAY / 22ᴺᴰ MAY

The Life of Our Father among the Saints

Beatus

(Second century)
Feast day 9th May / 22nd May

Little is known of Beatus and of his disciple Achates who are both celebrated today. He is honored as one of the Apostles of Switzerland and lived as a hermit on the slopes of the mountain which is named after him: Beatenberg, or the mountain of Beatus. The caves where he dwelt can be visited, the Beatushöhlen, situated close to Interlaken in the canton of Bern. The cave of St Beatus has become a tourist attraction where one may see a replica of his hermitage and his tomb.

According to tradition, St Beatus rid the area of a dragon, a feat which is represented on the shield of Beatenberg.

Saint Beatus, pray to God for us!

Troparion of the Hermits Saint Beatus and Saint Achates. Tone 4

Becoming hermits for the glory of God, / ye dwelt in self-denial and prayer. / In the spirit ye stood at the edge of heaven, / and after such lives devoted to Him, / ye were taken by Christ into His Kingdom. / Saints Beatus and Achates, pray to God for us.

15ᵀᴴ MAY / 28ᵀᴴ MAY

The Life of Our Father among the Saints

Paul II, Abbot of Saint Maurice of Agaunum and Successor to Paul I.

(† circa 550 A.D.)
Feast day 15ᵗʰ May / 28ᵗʰ May

Little is known of the life of St Paul II, but the chronicle of the abbots of the Monastery of Saint Maurice of Agaunum tells us that he had a great gift for miracles. Tradition relates that he raised a child from the dead whilst celebrating the Divine Liturgy.

Saint Paul, pray to God for us.

Troparion of Saint Paul II, Abbot of Saint Maurice of Agaunum. Tone 5

Working for the earthly glory of the Lord, / thou wast filled by Him with spiritual gifts, / and through Him thou didst work many miracles. / Thou didst even raise a child from the dead. / Abbot of the holy Monastery of Agaunum, / Saint Paul the second, pray to God for our souls.

15ᵀᴴ MAY / 28ᵀᴴ MAY

The Life of Our Father among the Saints

Paul I, Abbot of Saint Maurice of Agaunum

(+536 A.D.)
Feast day 15ᵗʰ May / 28ᵗʰ May

It is known that St Paul was the Abbot of the Monastery of Saint Maurice of Agaunum, but we have hardly any other details of his life. The chronicle of the Abbots of Agaunum states that he had great faith in God and worked miracles through his prayer. He cared for the poor and sheltered the orphans, and already in this life he had a vision of angels. He welcomed St Maur and his companions to Agaunum, who had come from St Benedict to spread the Benedictine Rule.

Saint Paul, pray to God for us!

Troparion of Saint Paul I, Abbot of Agaunum. Tone 6

Devoted to prayer and abstinence / and Abbot of the Monastery of Agaunum, / thou wast God's Providence for all the faithful. / Thou wast an angel in the flesh, / and God granted thee the vision of angels. / Holy Father Paul, pray to Christ our God to save our souls.

17ᵀᴴ MAY / 30ᵀᴴ MAY

The Life of Our Fathers among the Saints
Heradius, Paulinus, Aquilinus, Minerius, Victor, Artheme, Calcorus, Primus, Peregrinus, and Liberius.

(† circa 303 A.D.)
Feast day 17ᵗʰ May / 30ᵗʰ May

Up until the nineteenth century, the Diocese of Lausanne had four feasts dedicated to the different martyrs of Nyon. Only their first names were known and the fact they were martyred during the persecution of Diocletian. This second feast concerns those named above.

Before the Reformation, and before the occupation of the canton of Vaud by the Bernais (1536), the relics of all the martyrs of the town were exposed for the veneration of the faithful in the Church of Saint John the Baptist of Nyon. The town became a place of pilgrimage where miracles were worked through the Grace of God dwelling in the holy martyrs. Because of this veneration, the church was destroyed by the Protestants.

Holy martyrs of Nyon, pray to God for us!

Troparion of Saints Heradius, Paulinus, Aquilinus, Minerius, Victor, Artheme, Calcorus, Primus, Peregrinus, and Liberius, Martyrs of Nyon. Tone 5

Saints Heradius, Paulinus, Aquilinus, / with your companions Minerius and Victor, / Artheme, Calcorus, Primus, Liberius, and Peregrinus, / with great courage and strength in the Faith, / ye suffered martyrdom for Christ. / Now in the Kingdom of Heaven pray to God for us.

28ᵀᴴ MAY / 10ᵀᴴ JUNE

The Life of Our Father among the Saints
Thieteland, Co-adjudicator of Abbot Gregory of the Monastery of Einsiedeln
(✝ 960 A.D.)
Feast day 28ᵗʰ May / 10ᵗʰ June

Nothing more is known of the life of Thieteland other than he helped St Gregory with the administration, both spiritual and material, of the monastery of *Notre Dame des Ermites*.
   Saint Thieteland, pray to God for us!

Troparion of Saint Thieteland. Tone 3

Thou didst lead a pious life in Einsiedeln / before leaving for the Kingdom of God. / In self-denial, prayer and fasting, / thou didst help the abbot of the holy monastery / to care for his spiritual sheep. / Saint Thieteland, pray to God to save our souls.

29ᵀᴴ MAY / 11ᵀᴴ JUNE

The Life of Our Father among the Saints

Vital, Abbot of Saint Maurice of Agaunum and Successor to Saint Faustus

(† circa 515/516 A.D.)
Feast day 29ᵗʰ May / 11ᵗʰ June

Saint Vital was one of the companions of St Severin in France before he came to Switzerland. He was a chaste man, like an angel, and was responsible for the uncovering of the precious relics of Saints Severin, Faustus, Paschase, and Ursicin giving them a more honorable burial. He raised a girl from the dead who, according to tradition, later became a consecrated virgin. He left for Château-Landon where he departed to heaven on 29ᵗʰ May, close to the tomb of his master Severin.

Saint Vital, pray to God for us!

Troparion of Saint Vital, Abbot of Agaunum. Tone 6

Companion of the holy Abbot Severin, / thou didst follow him to the great Monastery of Agaunum. / Thou didst succeed Saint Faustus when his soul departed to God. / Man of prayer, thou didst work many miracles, / even raising a girl from the dead. / Holy Father Vital, pray to Christ our God to save our souls.

29ᵀᴴ MAY / 11ᵀᴴ JUNE

The Life of Our Father among the Saints

Ragnachaire, or Régnier, Bishop of Augst and of Basel

(† Seventh Century)
Feast day 29ᵗʰ May / 11ᵗʰ June

Ragnachaire (from Ragnachar, "powerful counselor") was a monk in the famous monastery of Luxeuil, founded by St

Columbanus. Later, he became bishop of the cities of Basel and Augst. Nothing more is known of his life. He departed to heaven sometime between 621 and 639.

Saint Ragnachaire, pray to God for us!

Troparion of Saint Ragnachaire, Bishop of Augst and Basel. Tone 5

Working for the earthly glory of the Lord, / thou didst wend thy way to the Heavenly Kingdom. / A monk of the great Saint Columbanus in Luxeuil, / thou didst leave the monastery at the call of God / to hold the see of Basel. / Saint Ragnachaire, pray to God for our salvation.

JUNE

3ʳᴰ June / 16ᵀᴴ June

The Life of Our Mother among the Saints
Clotilde, the Wife of King Clovis I
(545 A.D.)
Feast day 3ʳᵈ June / 16ᵗʰ June

The meek princess Clotilde (derived from the German *hlod* meaning "glory," and *hild* meaning "struggle") was the daughter of Chilperic, the King of Burgundy, and was born in Geneva in 474 or 475. She was taken captive by the Arian King Gondebaud who slew her father, but she kept her Orthodox Faith. When King Clovis I heard of her beauty and her pleasant character, he sent an emissary to Gondebaud in Geneva to ask for her hand in marriage, and his request was granted.

She became Queen of the Franks when she married Clovis circa 493 in Soissons, and through her meek example helped to convert him to Orthodox Christianity. He was baptized on the feast of the Nativity with his sister Alboflede between 496 and 499.

In 524, after the death of Clovis and one of her sons, Clodomir, she withdrew to pray at the tomb of St Martin of Tours. Clotilde, a most pious widow, founded many religious establishments. One of them is the Basilica of Saint Germain of Auxerre where

Clotilde
Femme de Clovis 1.ᵉ

Fig 19 Clotilde, second wife of Clovis I

archaeological research has shown that the building dates from her lifetime.

Another is the oratory close to Chelles dedicated to St George. At the end of his *History of the Franks, Book II*, St Gregory of Tours credits her with the foundation of the Royal Abbey of Saint Martin of Tours.

She ended her life in piety. Praying continuously at the tomb of the holy hierarch Martin of Tours, she received a revelation that she had only thirty more days to live. She spent them preparing herself for her departure to heaven, and died on 3ʳᵈ June / 16ᵗʰ

June 545. She was buried in Paris by her son Childebert beside her husband Clovis and his family. The tomb was in the sacristy of the Basilica of the Holy Apostles, which later became the Abbey of Saint Geneviève, whose founding was a result of her generosity.

Saint Clotilde, pray to God for us!

Troparion to the Holy Queen Clotilde. Tone 1

Bride of Clovis, / thou didst convert thy husband, / but as a widow thou didst see thy sons fall to slaying each other. / Thou didst then withdraw to Tours, / to the tomb of the holy Bishop Martin. / Thou didst end thine earthly life in the peace of the Lord. / Holy Queen Clotilde, pray to Him for our salvation.

8ᵀᴴ JUNE / 21ˢᵀ JUNE

The Lives of Our Fathers among the Saints
Eutychius, Attalus, Zoticus, Dinocus, Camsus, Quirinus, Julia, Saturnina, Galdunus, Ninnita, Fartunione, Cirinus, Ebustus, Rusticus, and Sylvius
(✝ 304 A.D.)
Feast day 8ᵗʰ June / 21ˢᵀ June

Up until the nineteenth century, the diocese of Lausanne celebrated four different feasts of the holy martyrs of Nyon. Only their first names were known and the fact they were martyred during the persecution of Diocletian. This third commemoration concerns the saints whose names are given above.

Before the Reformation, and before the occupation of the canton of Vaud by the Bernais (1536), in the Church of Saint John the Baptist of Nyon the relics of all the martyrs of the town were exposed for the veneration of the faithful. The town became a place of pilgrimage where miracles were worked through the Grace of God dwelling in the holy martyrs. Because of this veneration, the church was destroyed by the Protestants.

Holy martyrs of Nyon, pray to God for us!

Troparion of Saints Eutychius, Attalus, Zoticus, Dinocus, Camsus, Quirinus, Julia, Saturnina, Galdunus, Ninnita, Fartunione, Sirius, Ebustus, Rusticus, and Sylvain, Martyrs of Nyon. Tone 5

Saints Euthychius, Attalus, Zoticus, and Dinocus, / Camsus, Quirinus, Julia, Saturnina, Galdunus, and Ninnita, / Fartunione, Sirius, Ebustus, Rusticus, and Sylvain,/ and all other Christians firm in the Faith, / ye suffered martyrdom for Christ, / pray now to God in heaven for our souls.

9ᵀᴴ JUNE / 22ᴺᴰ JUNE

The Lives of Our Fathers among the Saints

Amantius, Lucius, Alexander, Donatus, Peregrinus, and Andrew

(† 304 A.D.)
Feast day 9ᵗʰ June / 22ⁿᵈ June

Up until the nineteenth century the diocese of Lausanne celebrated four different feasts of the holy martyrs of Nyon. Only their first names were known and the fact they were martyred during the persecution of Diocletian. This fourth commemoration concerns the saints whose names are given above.

Before the Reformation, and before the occupation of the canton of Vaud by the Bernais (1536), in the Church of Saint John the Baptist of Nyon the relics of all the martyrs of the town were exposed for the veneration of the faithful. The town became a place of pilgrimage where miracles were worked through the Grace of God dwelling in the holy martyrs. Because of this veneration, the church was destroyed by the Protestants.

Holy martyrs of Nyon, pray to God for us!

Troparion of Saints Amantius, Lucius, Alexander, Donatus, Peregrinus, and Andrew, Martyrs of Nyon. Tone 5

Saints Amantius, Lucius, Alexander, and Andrew, / and your brothers, Donatus and Peregrinus, / ye fought the good fight for Christ, / and with courage and firm faith / ye gave your lives for the Lord. / Pray for us before the heavenly throne.

9ᵀᴴ JUNE / 22ᴺᴰ JUNE

The Life of Our Father among the Saints
Asinius (or Asimo), First Bishop of Coire
(†451 A.D.)
Feast day 9th June / 23rd June

Asinius (or Asimo) lived in the fifth century and was one of the first, if not the very first, Bishops of Coire. He is mentioned in a document as having been present at the Council of Milan.

Holy Father Asinius, pray to God for us!

Troparion of Saint Asinius, Bishop of Coire. Tone 1

Thou wast one of the first bishops in the Grisors, / and did attend the Council of Milan. / Before departing into the Kingdom of the Lord, / thou wast a good shepherd of the Orthodox Church, / bringing to Christ thy spiritual sheep. / Saint Asinius, pray to God to save our souls.

JULY

The Lives of Our Fathers among the Saints

Placide and Sigisbert, Monks and Martyrs

(✝630 A.D.)
Feast day 11ᵗʰ July / 24ᵗʰ July

Saint Sigisbert, or Sigebert, came from Ireland to become a monk at Luxeuil. He followed St Columbanus toward Italy, but only as far as Disentis in the Grisors. There he built a chapel. Other monks joined him, and he became their abbot.

Not far from there was a castle called Tremisium, which was the dwelling of a rich and powerful man called Placide. One day, his curiosity led him to attend and listen to the preaching of the saint. Overcome by his holy eloquence, Placide fell at his feet and asked for baptism.

Sigisbert joyfully agreed. He instructed him in the holy mysteries of the faith and baptized him. Soon, Placide wished to imitate the example of the holy abbot. Desiring to live a more perfect life, he gave all his possessions to God and His Most Pure Mother, and was tonsured with the monastic habit by Sigisbert, his spiritual father.

On the lands given by Placide, Sigisbert founded a holy monastery. However, when Placide joined the monastery, the Governor of the Province, Victor, became irritated at the founding of a foreign monastery which he felt was a danger to the independence of Raetia. Worse, he was infuriated by Sigisbert's reproaches for his dissolute life. As a result, he had Placide murdered on 11th July / 24th July 630 by having his head cut off—just as Herod had beheaded St John the Baptist. Not long afterwards, Victor was drowned in an accident in the Rhine, and the Monastery of Disentis prospered.

Sigisbert did not survive his holy disciple for long. He departed to heaven in 636 and was buried in the tomb of his friend. An ancient inscription proclaims: "The same grave unites in death those who cultivated together their virtues in life."

Saints Placide and Sigisbert, pray to God for us!

Troparion of Saints Placide and Sigisbert, Martyrs. Tone 5

Saint Sigisbert thou didst found in the Grisors a holy monastery, / where, by thy preaching, thou didst convert Placide / and tonsured him monk. / Reproaching the local Herod, thou wast martyred. / Afterward thy disciple, Placide, didst join you in the heavenly kingdom. / Saints Sigisbert and Placide, pray to God for us.

22ND JULY / 4TH AUGUST

The Life of Our Father among the Saints
Wandrille, Evangelist of Switzerland and Abbot of Fontenelle
(† 668 A.D.)
Feast day 22nd July / 4th August

Wandrille was born into a noble family. He was the son of Duke Walchise and Princess Doda, the daughter of Bishop Arnould of Metz, and was a page in the court of King Dagobert I of the Franks.

He married and was appointed Count of the Palace, but after a while the two spouses agreed to separate. Wandrille resigned

Fig 20 Statue of Saint Wandrille, Abbot of Fontenelle

from all his positions in the Palace and left to become a monk, wandering in search of salvation for his soul. He stayed at Montfaucon in France, at Saint-Ursanne in Switzerland, and at Bobbio in Italy. Wandrille even traveled Ireland. He then returned to Switzerland, to Romainmôtier, where he remained for ten years.

He stayed for four years at Saint-Ursanne, and took part in the building of the monastery, leaving his spiritual stamp on the holy place.

Afterwards, he was sent to Normandy by St Ouen who ordained him priest. He then founded the Abbey of Fontenelle in the Forest of Jumieges and became its abbot. Later, the abbey was named after him.

Wandrille was a man of great faith and a tireless pilgrim of Christ. He served God and his flock with kindness, not caring for the vain riches of this world. Rather, he sought for the great treasures of the Gospel and lived by them throughout his blessed life, imparting them to the hearts of those who came into contact with him.

He lived to a great age in self-denial and toil. Death held no terrors for him for he believed firmly that it would bring that rest in God which he had so long desired. Tradition relates that as his life drew to a close, he often sighed, crying out like the Psalmist: "Alas, how long is my exile, and for how long has my soul been a stranger on earth" (see Ps 118:19–20 LXX).

At last, God heard his prayer and sent an illness which brought about his deliverance. For three days and three nights he was sick, entering into an ecstasy where he saw heaven.

Wandrille gave excellent spiritual teaching to his disciples and predicted several future events to them. He predicted that St Lambert (later Bishop of Toulouse), and St Ansbert (who succeeded St Ouen as Bishop of Rouen) would succeed him as abbots of the monastery. He communed piously of the Holy Gifts and then died in the presence of Ouen, his archbishop. He was also surrounded by three hundred of his monks, all in tears at the loss of such a good father. He departed to heaven on 22^(nd) July / 4^(th) August 668.

Holy Father Wandrille, pray to God for us!

Troparion of Saint Wandrille, Abbot, and Founder of Fontenelle. Tone 7

Thou wast Count of the Palace of King Dagobert / and didst live in chastity with thy wife. / Then thou wast professed a monk / at Montfaucon in Champagne / before founding the Abbey of Fontenelle / and preaching in the land of Caux. / Saint Wandrille, pray to Christ our God to save our souls.

AUGUST

The Lives of Our Fathers among the Saints,
the Abbots of Agaunum:
**Venerand († 536 A.D.), Ambrose I († 520 A.D.),
Paul I († 544 A.D.), Jucondinus († circa 600 A.D.),
Secundinus († 622 A.D.), and Récolème
(† circa 640 A.D.)**
Feast day 1ˢᵗ August / 14ᵗʰ August

Saint Venerand

Tradition relates that Venerand was a native of Agaunum who from his childhood spent whole days in the Monastery of Saint Maurice, thus preparing himself for life as a monk. He was professed a monk and became Abbot in 530 as successor to St Tranquillinus. He was a great example of Christian virtues and watched over his monks until he departed to heaven in 536.

Saint Venerand pray to God for us!

Saint Ambrose I

(2ⁿᵈ November / 15ᵗʰ November, see page 27)

Saint Paul I

(15th May / 28th May, see page 89)

Saint Jucondinus

Little is known of this holy abbot. Jucondinus welcomed King Gontran to the monastery when he visited the Valais with Bishop Heliodorus of Sion. A supernatural revelation led all three of them to take part in the discovery of the relics of Saints Amator and Viator, martyrs of the Theban Legion.

Saint Jucondinus, pray to God for us!

Saint Secundinus

Secundinus was an abbot during the reign of Clothaire II. Nothing else is known of him.

Saint Secundinus, pray to God for us!

Saint Récolème

Récolème was Abbot of Saint Maurice, unfortunately nothing else is known of his life.

Saint Récolème, pray to God for us!

Troparion of the Holy Abbots of Agaunum. Tone 5

Saint Venerand, St Ambrose, and Saint Paul, the first of that name, / Saint Jucondinus, Saint Secundinus, and Saint Récolème / all Abbots of Agaunum, / ye did lead the prayer of your monks / to the threshold of the Kingdom of the Lord. / Holy and pious Abbots, pray to God for our souls.

3ᴿᴰ August / 16ᵀᴴ August

The Life of Our Father among the Saints
Benno (Benedict, or Bennon)
(† 940 A.D.)
Feast day 3ʳᵈ August / 16ᵗʰ August

Saint Benno came from Swabia. He was related to Raoul, King of Burgundy, and was a canon of Strasburg. Later in life he withdrew to a desert place several leagues[47] from Zurich where forty-three years before St Meinard had founded a monastery which was later to become the Abbey of Einsiedeln. In this place of deep prayer his body was nourished by a few wild herbs and berries, and his soul more richly by prayer and self-denial. After some time, disciples came to share his highly spiritual life and to clear the surrounding forest.

"Faith must bear the fruits of life to guide the ascetic to eternal life," as states the monastic tradition. Benno and his disciples made great strides along this path of Christian perfection. The lord of the region, seeing their holy life, ceded to them some land in the wilderness. They made good use of it, rebuilding the ruined chapel and building several cells which were to grow into the famous Abbey of the Hermits of Our Lady in Einsiedeln.

In this manner a numerous community grew up around the holy man. Their sole rule was the example of the holy life of St Benno until later, when the rule of St Benedict was introduced. The Abbey of Seckingen granted the Isle of Uffnau as a dependence to Einsiedeln.

Benno had left the world with the resolve never to return. He had found in the desert an ample reward for all the sacrifices he had willingly accepted. But the King,[48] Henry the Fowler, tore him away from the desert to place him in the see of Metz. He had heard of the holiness of St Benno and of his great qualities, admired by all, and so appointed him to rule the Church in that city.

The servant of God sorrowfully yielded to the decree of the king. "The idea that God could be glorified in this eminent position was the only argument which made him yield," states one of his biographers. He left his monastery in 923. His disciples were inconsolable at this loss, but Benno calmed their pain by promising to return in due time.

Benno applied himself with apostolic zeal to heal the wounds of his church. Truly, there was great disorder which had led the king to appoint him to this charge. But ungrateful and unruly folk are not easy to lead in the way of salvation, and it was only through the great and manifest virtues of the holy hierarch that the hostility of his flock could be restrained. To the threats of violence, Benno replied with the meekness and holiness of his life: night and day he prayed to Christ to grant him the patience to overcome the rebellious souls of his flock. Despite the hostility of his flock, the righteous bishop rebuked forcefully all the vices he found in his church. As a result, in 927, several criminals who were offended at his holy zeal seized him and put out his eyes, "mutilating him in the most shameful fashion."

Benno bore these cruel deeds with a martyr's courage. Though he knew his attackers, he sought no vengeance and would not deliver them to the king's justice—he even asked that they be pardoned. The Council of Duisburg pronounced a sentence of excommunication against the guilty ones and punished them according to the laws then in force. The blessed hierarch resigned his see and set out once more for his desert. His former disciples received him with reverence and treated him as a martyr.

Benno considered this trial from heaven to be a blessing from the Lord. By losing bodily sight, he gained from God the means to advance further on the path of virtue. During the ten years which remained to him, he spent his whole life in pious works and ascetic labors.

He never ceased from giving the holy example of complete obedience to the Will of God. One of his biographers states: "He could truly say in the spirit of the great Apostle of olden times: Who shall separate us from the love of Christ? Crowns, riches, and pleasures, these charms have I trampled underfoot. Tribulations, temptations of all kinds, troubles of body and soul have never shaken my steadfastness; and thou, O death, who seemest so dreadful, thy blows do I despise. I fear them not, for I hope in one greater than thee: in the One who destroyed thine empire and took away thy prey."

Benno never complained of the sad condition in which his wounds had left him. He was occupied with spiritual things and his monks often sought his advice on their way toward perfection.

Toward the end of his life, the pious hierarch succumbed to various illnesses above and beyond his usual trials. Yet, in the midst of the most painful sufferings, one might often hear him speak these wondrous words: "O Lord, increase my sufferings but grant me patience." He calmly prepared for death in a fine and holy conversation with God.

At last, after long years as the living example of all the virtues for his disciples, he gave his blessed soul to the Lord on 3rd August / 16th August 940, in the arms of St Evrard (see his life, page 112) and embraced by the love of them all.

Saint Benno, pray to God for us!

Troparion of Saint Benno, Monk, and Bishop of Metz. Tone 5

Thou didst travel toward the Heavenly Kingdom, / at first a monk, then ordained a bishop to restore the Church in the see of Metz. / The evil ones blinded and mutilated thee / but thou forgavest them and became once more a monk. / Saint Benno, thou who art good, pray to God to save our souls.

14ᵀᴴ AUGUST / 27ᵀᴴ AUGUST

The Life of Our Father among the Saints

Evrard (or Eberhard), Abbot of Einsiedeln

(† 958 A.D.)

Feast day 14ᵗʰ August / 27ᵗʰ August

Saint Evrard was a count, a member of a noble family of Swabia and cousin of Hermann, the Duke of Swabia and Alsace. Like St Benno he was a priest of the Diocese of Strasbourg. He became Provost of the Cathedral of Strasburg, then joined St Benno of Metz in the famous Monastery of Einsiedeln in Switzerland, where formerly hermits had dwelt.

Benno persuaded him of the vanity of a life in the world and through his example, encouraged him to embark on a more spiritual life. For before that, Evrard had been dazzled and fascinated by the pomp of the great things of the world and greatly attracted to vainglory.

It was through curiosity that he went to visit this man who had abandoned his position to live in the desert. Benno welcomed him simply. His evident joy in the austere and lonely desert first intrigued Evrard, then opened his eyes. He told his friend that he was converted, and Benno urged him completely to renounce the world. Evrard did so, leaving behind his responsibilities and his goods. He used his wealth to finish the construction of the monastery and became its first abbot.

The humble chapel rebuilt by Benno and his disciples was replaced by a beautiful church, built in honor of the Most Holy Mother of God, and the humble cells of the monks were replaced by the cloisters of a rich abbey which was to become famous.

However, the charity of Evrard became still more evident during the great famine which struck Burgundy, Alsace, and Upper Germany in 942. He sent great quantities of grain to the famished and suffering folk. He was elected abbot of the monastery which he had built in 934 and from then on, he guided this haven of God until his departure to heaven, in 957 or 958 on 14th August / 27th August.

He was buried close to the Chapel of the Mother of God, beside his friend and brother St Benno, and by the famous Church of *Notre Dame des Ermites* (Our Lady of the Hermits).

Saint Evrard, pray to God for us.

Troparion of Saint Evrard, First Abbot of *Notre Dame des Ermites*. Tone 6

Son of Swabia and priest in the city of Strasbourg, / thou didst visit Saint Benno in the desert. / He persuaded thee to leave this vain world, / and thou didst finish building the monastery / of which thou wast elected the first abbot. / Saint Evrard, pray to Christ our God to have mercy on us.

Fig 21 Saint Theodore of Martigny

16TH AUGUST / 29TH AUGUST

The Life of Our Father among the Saints

Theodore (Sometimes Called Theodoulos) of Martigny

(Fourth Century)
Feast day 16th August / 29th August

Theodore, the holy Bishop of Martigny (then known as Octodurum) was most likely of Greek descent. He was born during the first years of the fourth century and was raised in faith and piety from his childhood.

By virtue of his gifts for the spiritual life, God called him to the priesthood. Theodore was an example of faith and righteousness. He was ordained bishop of the Valais around 349 and is the first bishop of this see known to us. It is thought that he was sent by St Protais, Bishop of Milan, and Metropolitan of the Valais.

He established himself at Martigny, the chief city of the Alps, and there he dwelt. Whilst he was bishop, his beneficial influence caused pagan rites to disappear; and the crude customs and superstitions of those who lived there gave way to a Christian life more in keeping with the Gospel.

The holy hierarch was not simply the Bishop of Martigny but a missionary as well. He was an apostle to what then was known as Lesser Burgundy, the present-day Swiss Romandie and parts of the Cantons of Bern and Soleure. Nothing could stop him in his holy mission of preaching the faith according to one of his biographers. His name is mentioned in the acts of the Council of Aquila held in 381 to condemn the Arian heresy. Theodore sat beside the famous St Ambrose of Milan in this assembly which drove two Arian bishops from the Church. The account of the council has preserved Theodore's opinion: "Palladius (one of the bishops judged by the Council), who has denied that Christ is truly God and coeternal with His Father, is no longer recognized as either Christian or Priest."

Several years later, in 393, another heresy threatened the Church of Christ. A former monk, Jovinian, who had left his monastery to lead an unedifying life, started to preach that the ascetic life was useless together with a false doctrine of the Mother of God and depravity in morals. Once again, St Ambrose assembled a Council to which our Holy Father Theodore came as a zealous guardian of the faith.

But the greatest glory of St Theodore was to have discovered the relics of the martyrs of Agaunum. Some of the saints he discovered through divine revelation, others through the witness of Christians who had seen the martyrdom. In the end, he found a great number of relics of the Holy Legion of Christ martyred for the faith at Agaunum.

After the sacred uncovering of those who had watered the land of the Valais in Switzerland with their blood, the holy bishop had a church built to house the precious remains of the martyred Christian army.

Tradition relates that many of those who dwelt there brought a stone for the building of the humble church of the martyrs. The masons who built the church stopped working on Sundays to respect the day of the Lord. However one of them, a pagan, continued his work while the others went to the divine service. He was stopped in his tracks by a company of the martyrs who appeared to him surrounded by a brilliant light. Terrified, he fled as fast as his legs would carry him to join his comrades in the church and beg for immediate baptism.

After the church was finished, pilgrims started to come from all over Gaul, and the holy bishop encouraged the cult of the saints to spread by giving some of the relics to various holy people of that time, among them St Victrix of Rouen, St Ambrose of Milan, and St Martin of Tours. Later, many towns placed themselves under the protection of the holy martyrs of the Valais, and of Saint-Maurice in particular, one of whose arms was taken to a church in Prague.

Saint Theodore did not simply house the holy remains of the martyrs in a holy place. He also worked to spread abroad the account of their lives and deeds. It is known that he informed the first Bishop of Geneva, St Isaac, of the acts of the pious legion, and through St Isaac, St Eucher of Lyon learnt of them.

After a holy life of prayer, of spiritual warfare for the faith, and of authentic Christian self-denial, the pious hierarch of Christ, Theodore, died and was buried in Sion, for he had clearly transferred his see to that city.

Saint Theodore, pray to God for us!

Troparion of Saint Theodore, Bishop of Martigny and Discoverer of the Relics of the Holy Martyrs of Agaunum. Tone 1

Thou wast the first bishop of Martigny, / and with Saint Ambrose didst take part in the Councils of Aquila and of Milan. / Through thee, the holy relics of the martyrs of Agaunum were discovered for veneration. / And thou didst make them known to all Christians. / Holy Father Theodore, pray to God to save our souls.

28ᵗʰ August / 10ᵗʰ September

The Life of Our Father among the Saints
Pelagius of Constance
(† circa 283 A.D.)
Feast day 28ᵗʰ August / 10ᵗʰ September

All that is known of St Pelagius is that he was martyred around 280 during the reign of Numerian, and that from very early times he was adopted as the holy patron of the city of Constance.

Saint and martyr Pelagius, pray to God for us!

Troparion of Saint Pelagius. Tone 8

Perfect disciple of our Lord Jesus, / thou didst live by His holy commandments, / and when thou wast taken by impious men / thou wast tortured to make thee deny the faith / and so received from Christ baptism in thy blood. / Saint Pelagius, pray to God to have mercy upon us.

Feast Days of the Saints of Helvetia

Notker the Stammerer.............................6 / 19 Apr

Nyon, The Holy Martyrs of ....17 / 30 May & 8/24 Jun

Othmar, Abbot of Saint Gall ....16 / 29 Nov

Oyend, Abbot of Condat ....1 / 14 Jan

Pantalus, Martyr of Basel ....16 / 29 Oct

Paul I, Abbot of Agaunum ....15 / 28 May

Paul II, Abbot of Agaunum ....15 / 28 May

Pelagius of Constance ....28 Aug /10 Sep

Pirmin, Abbot of Hornbach........................3 / 16 Nov

Placide, Martyr ....11 Jul / 24 Jul

Protais, Bishop of Lausanne.........................6 / 19 Nov

Ragnachaire, Bishop of Basel ....29 May / 11 Jun

Randoald, Martyr.................................21 Feb / 5 Mar

Récolème, Abbot of Agaunum ....1 / 14 Aug

Regula of the Theban Legion........................11 / 24 Sep

Romanus of Condat...............................28 Feb / 12 Mar

Salonius of Geneva................................28 Sep / 11 Oct

Secundinus, Abbot of Agaunum......................1 / 14 Aug

Severin, Abbot of Agaunum.........................11 /24 Feb

Sigisbert, Monk ....11 Jul / 24 Jul

Sigismond, King of Burgundy........................1 / 14 May

Theodore, Bishop of Martigny ....16 /29 Aug

Thieteland of Einsiedeln ....28 May / 10 Jun

Tranquillinus, Abbot of Agaunum ....12 / 25 Dec

Tutilon, Monk of Saint-Gall ....28 Mar /10 Apr

Ursannus, Disciple of Saint Columbanus..............16 / 29 Dec

Ursicin, Abbot of Disentiss ....2 / 15 Oct

Ursus, Martyr River Aar ....30 Sep / 13 Oct

Valentinian, Bishop of Coire ....7 / 20 Jan

Venerand, Abbot of Agaunum.......................1 / 14 Aug

Verena of Zurzach.................................1 / 14 Sep

Victor, Martyr River Aar ....30 Sep / 13 Oct

Vital, Abbot of Agaunum ....29 May / 11 Jun

Wandrille, Abbot of Fontenelle ....22 Jul / 4 Aug

Wiborade, Virgin and Martyr ....1 / 14 May

Ynnemod, Abbot of Agaunum.......................11 / 24 Jan

Yole of La Balme ....28 Feb / 12 Mar

SERVICE TO ALL THE SAINTS
Who Shone Forth in Switzerland

Commemorated on the 3rd Sunday of September
according to the civil calendar[49]

Great Vespers

On Lord I have cried, these stichera in the 4th Tone:

O ye faithful people let us sing to the glory of the martyrs who have reddened with their blood the banner next to the bright cross of Christ. As true soldiers of Christ the glorious legion fought until death to gain immortal life; and we pray them that their blood may water the dry earth of our souls that they may bring forth the grace of salvation.

O ye holy bishops of the land of the Swiss, ye spared no pain or labor to build the unshakeable wall of faith, and to build in the souls of your flock the temple of the Holy Spirit. And now we pray, O builders of the Church, to lay the cornerstone of the salvation in our souls.

O ye holy hermits and ascetics, it was with the tools of fasting, vigil, and prayer, that ye did plough and enrich the land of the Swiss, to sow there the good seed and bring forth the fruit of faith. And now, as faithful stewards, ye tend the harvest by praying for the salvation of our souls before the throne of the Lord.

Doxastikon in the 6th Tone:

Today Switzerland giveth thanks to her Master, for the cross which she did bear as a standard hath protected her from sorrows and trials. Today the martyrs of Agaunum rejoice with the righteous. Marius, Protais, Salonius and all the hierarchs sing with the choir of the Apostles. The hermits of the Jura exult with the prophets, and we mix our voices with the song of the Angels to praise the Creator of all things and beseech him for the salvation of our souls.

Both now. . .
The Dogmatic Theotokion of the week.

Aposticha from the Octoechos.

Doxastikon in the 4th Tone:

As we celebrate the yearly memorial of our holy countrymen, let us praise them worthily. In truth they knew all the beatitudes of the Lord: poor, they were rich in spirit; meek, they inherited the earth; mourning, they were comforted; hungering for righteousness, they were filled; merciful, they received mercy; pure in heart, they saw God as far as they were able; peacemakers, they became children of God; persecuted for righteousness sake, they are now filled with heavenly joy and pray the Lord without ceasing to have mercy on our land.

Troparion, in the 8th Tone:

As the ripe fruit of Thy saving seed, the land of the Swiss bringeth Thee, O Lord, all the saints who flourished there. By their prayers keep Thy Church and our land in deep peace, through the power of Thy Cross, O Merciful One.

Matins

Canon

Canticle One

Refrain: Saints of Switzerland, pray to God for us.

Obeying the earthly king, O Maurice, thou didst lead thy legion from far-off Egypt to Switzerland; but there it was for the Heavenly King that thou didst fight to the death with thy companions.

Rather than obey the wicked command of the tyrant, the glorious legion of martyrs laid down its weapons of steel, and through the spiritual weapon of faith the Thebans gained incorruptible crowns.

The blood of the six thousand companions of Maurice, Candide and Innocent reddened the waters of the Rhone. As a sacred treasure, the river carried down to the great sea the tidings of the victory of the soldiers of Christ.

Theotokion: O Virgin Mother of God, hope of Christians, grant us also thy mercy as to our fathers in the days of old. Keep us and protect us from all evil.

Canticle Three

Not a single legionary faltered at Agaunum in the dread combat, but it pleased the Lord to send some of the faithful Thebans to bear the news of salvation elsewhere.

Ursus and Victor, ye received the veteran Vincent at Soleure to teach him the Gospel. The tyrant desired to blot out even your memory by casting your tortured remains into the river; but the Lord drew you out from thence to show forth His Glory at your graves.

And thou, O Exupery, wast hidden in Zurich by the pious Felix and Regula; but since the Word of Truth cannot be hidden, with joy they were partakers in the martyrdom of the Theban.

Theotokion: Behold, the time hath come to fly to our help, O Most Holy Mother of God, for our temptations increase; now is the time, O brothers, when we sigh for her. Let us all say with our whole heart: Queen, O Heavenly Queen, come to the aid of Thy people.

Kontakion in the 4ᵗʰ Tone:

When he found the place which Thou hadst chosen for his sobriety, / Gall raised up the cross and sang to Thee: / O Lord Jesus Christ, Who hath saved mankind on a Cross, / grant that this place may be holy to Thee / and ever resound with the songs of Thy praise.

Ikos:

Come, O ye faithful, let us join our voices to those of Maurice and his companions, of the holy hierarchs and hermits, to beseech the Master of all for the salvation of our souls, that the land of the Swiss which He protecteth with His Precious Cross may ever resound with the song of His praise.

Canticle Four

With Athanasius, the dauntless confessor of Alexandria. Hilary the friend of great Basil and Gregory, Ambrose, the Bishop of Milan, and Martin the wonderworker of Tours, the whole Church came to venerate the divine martyrs offered up by the land of the Swiss.

After founding the Church of Basel, O Pantalus, thou wast a watchful pastor for thy flock. When Saint Ursula and her companions arrived in thy city, thou didst receive them worthily as holy pilgrims, before going with the holy virgins to their martyrdom.

O Theodore, thou wast a tireless apostle of the see to which thou wast ordained, for thou didst bear the Gospel into its deepest valleys. And thus thou wast found worthy to find the relics of Maurice and the Thebans and to build the sanctuary for their veneration.

Theotokion: O Virgin Mother of God, hope of Christians, grant us also thy mercy as to our fathers in the days of old. Keep us and protect us from all evil.

Canticle Five

From thy childhood, O Marius, thou wast pledged to the Lord, dedicating to Him thy riches and thy works. He granted the Church of Lausanne to thy wisdom which shone forth during times of trouble.

With the legacy of thy father thou didst build churches, O holy hierarch Marius, and with thine own hands didst fashion their chalices. Thy pastoral zeal brought the Word of Truth to the furthest reaches of thy see. There thou didst meet the holy hermit Pontius whom thou didst make guide to the monasteries which thou hadst founded in the Jura.

Choosing nakedness, fasting, and prayer, thou didst care for the unfortunate, feed the hungry, and console the afflicted, O Marius, true shepherd of the sheep entrusted to thee by Christ.

O Protais, thou wast the worthy successor of the holy bishop Marius, for after placing thy city in the care of the Mother of God, thou didst die caring for the poorest of thy flock.

Theotokion: Thou art the Immaculate Temple of God Whom nothing can contain, O Heavenly Queen. By thy prayers grant that we who entreat thee may likewise be temples of the grace of God.

Canticle Six

O Salonius, thou wast the adornment of the Church of Geneva. Tireless herald of the Gospel, thou didst teach the Word to thy people, an example of Orthodox piety for them all.

O Clotilde, most blessed saint, before enlightening thy royal spouse with the Faith, thou didst joyfully welcome to thy native city the relics of Saint Victor, the holy protector of Geneva.

O holy King Sigismond, the Truth was thy foremost care. Thou didst escape the nets of heresy, and as a faithful disciple of Avit, the holy bishop of Lyon, thou didst turn thy kingdom again to Orthodoxy.

Theotokion: By thy prayers, O Holy Mother of God, may we be delivered from our sins to receive, O Pure Virgin, the divine enlightenment of thy Son Who took flesh in thy womb.

Resurrectional Kontakion and Ikos in the tone of the week.

Canticle Seven

Land of the Swiss, rejoice, for thou wast trodden by the feet of Lucius, Eremita and Placide, Ursanne, Pirmin, Beatus and Verena, and the rest of the ascetics and hermits. Sing therefore with them: blessed art Thou, O God of our fathers.

From his capital, Geneva, the pious King Sigismond went to Agaunum to raise there a monastery to the glory of the Theban martyrs; and there he ordained the ceaseless song: blessed art Thou, O God of our fathers.

Germain, the holy Abbot of Grandval with his faithful companion Randoald bore witness to righteousness unto blood before the tyrant whose blind impiety made him a murderer. But his saintly daughter, Odile, her blindness healed by the prayers of the holy martyrs, opened the eyes of her father to repentance so that he could cry out: blessed art Thou, O God of our fathers.

Theotokion: O most blessed virgin, thou art truly the branch which sprang from the root of Jesse to give birth to the Fruit of salvation for the faithful who cry out to thy Son: blessed art Thou, O God of our fathers.

Canticle Eight

When the thick clouds of pagan darkness still covered our land, Columbanus, Gall, and their companions, with Fridolin crossed the sea to teach us to sing with them: O all ye works of the Lord, bless ye the Lord: praise and exalt him above all for ever.

O Fridolin thou didst fervently wish to venerate the relics of Saint Hilary, the true confessor of the Faith, and at Poitiers thy master didst appear to thee, to tell thee to awaken the faith of the Allemans. Thus, O holy missionary, thou didst give thy name to the valley of Glaris, that it should sing with thee: O all ye works of the Lord, bless ye the Lord: praise and exalt him above all for ever.

Neither threats, nor trials, nor cold, nor wild beasts could drive thee from the place which God had chosen, O Gall, holy pilgrim of the Gospel. So the people of Austrasia returned to God and sang with thee: O all ye works of the Lord, bless ye the Lord: praise and exalt him above all for ever.

Theotokion: O Virgin who, in ways past understanding, didst bring forth God the Word, Creator and Saviour, thee do we praise unto ages of ages.

Canticle Nine

O mountains of the Jura, ye were a Thebaid where flourished a great company of monks, hermits, and ascetics. From your heights rose up the voices of our holy fathers, bringing before the throne of God the praise and thanksgiving of Switzerland.

Imier, thou didst leave thy native land to know the birthplace of the Lord. There thou wast the trusty disciple of the Patriarch of the mother of the Churches. Then thou didst return to teach thy countrymen of the splendour of the Holy Places and the all-powerful glory of salvation.

Romanus, thou didst live according to the Word of the Creator. In the thick forest thou didst clear a monastic paradise with Lupicinus, thy brother in the flesh and in self-denial. With Yole, your sister, ye led a great company of the faithful on the way of salvation.

Your clairvoyance and charity, love of neighbour and gift of healing made ye shine like stars, O holy fathers Romanus and Lupicinus; and the splendour of your miracles enlighteneth the land of the Swiss.

Theotokion: Hilarion, the holy hierarch of Poitiers, teacher of Truth, teacheth his Swiss disciples to glorify thus the Mother of God: The Virgin, her birthgiving, the Son born of her, the Cross, death, and the descent into hell: these brought us salvation. For the sake of the human race the Son of God was well pleased to be born of the Virgin and the Holy Spirit.

Exapostilarion:

Let us praise in songs the unquenchable lights of Switzerland, vessels of the Divine Word. By glorifying Christ Who didst love and enlighten them we gain them as intercessors for our souls.

Composed by Bishop Ambrose (Cantacuzène) of Vevey

AKATHIST TO ALL THE SAINTS
Who Have Enlightened the Land of the Swiss

Kontakion 1

The land of the Swiss dwelt in the dark depths of paganism, but the Gospel was spread abroad by different messengers, both men and women from different lands; and the Good News of the Light of Christ arose suddenly, as a spiritual dawn, bringing in the new mankind to whom we cry: Rejoice, all ye saints of Switzerland.

Ikos 1

Holy Fathers, holy Mothers, from the dawn of your preaching your spiritual struggle was victorious against the depth of ignorance and the violence rooted in those captive souls, bringing them on a path of light to the haven of salvation in Christ through the sacraments, so we cry to you:

Rejoice Saints Beatus and Achates!

Rejoice Saint Maurice and thy soldiers!

Rejoice Saints Oyend and Meinrad!

Rejoice Saints Sigismond and Clotilde!

Rejoice Saints Tutilon and Notker!

Rejoice, all ye Saints of Switzerland!

Kontakion 2

Zealous missionaries of the Kingdom of God, exiled far from your native lands, in the land of the living ye chose to be links in a golden chain which riseth up to heaven where ye now all sing: Alleluia!

Ikos 2

Eternity is the present, blessed by God, where spreadeth out the splendid kingdom of souls, freed from their earthly burden and the foolish cares of the world which crush the spirit, and which hinder them from reaching the one thing needful. Fathers and Mothers among the saints ye have chosen the better part and we cry to you:

Rejoice Saints Eusebius and Adelric!

Rejoice Saints Benno and Theodore!

Rejoice Saints Protais and Evrard!

Rejoice Saints Amé and Salonius!

Rejoice Saints Ursus and Victor!

Rejoice all ye Saints of Switzerland!

Kontakion 3

In this worldly tower of Babel, ye chose the universal tongue of prayer whilst yet remaining Gauls, Germans, Romansh, or Latins with all those who heard your preaching, proclaiming to them in their own tongues the mysteries of the Faith. For ye wished to save their souls for God, singing: Alleluia!

Ikos 3

Clearing the thick forests in the lands where ye struggled, in holy ways ye uprooted the thorns of sin and broke the bonds of the devil who held captive your future flock in heathen darkness. So we cry to you with thanks:

Rejoice Saints Fintan and Othmar!

Rejoice Saints Fridolin and Theodore!

Rejoice Saints Severin and Magnus!

Rejoice Saints Achive and Severin!

Rejoice Saints Pantalus and Ursula!

Rejoice all ye Saints of Switzerland!

Kontakion 4

Fishers of men and women, cultivators of souls lying fallow, ye spared neither your zeal nor your lives to bring those lost in the night of unbelief and superstition to the saving cradle of Christ. Saving them, ye sang to God: Alleluia!

Ikos 4

The kings of this world, recalling that beyond the grave they would no more be crowned, often helped you to fulfill your mission for the Church. She therefore also honors them as saints, and to them the land of the Swiss giveth thanks: Saints of God Sigismond, Gontran and Clovis, sing with us the glory of the sons and daughters of our land:

Rejoice Saints Lucius and Emerita!

Rejoice Saint Placide and Sigisbert!

Rejoice Saints Romanus and Lupicinus!

Rejoice Saint Germain and Randoald!

Rejoice Saints Columbanus and Gall!

Rejoice all ye Saints of Switzerland!

Kontakion 5

Neither hunger nor thirst, nor trials nor tortures, nor even death could deflect you from your holy mission. Your whole being was given to the one thing needful: the coming of the Kingdom. Bringing the people of this land to confess Christ God, ye sang to Him: Alleluia!

Ikos 5

In the wild places of the deserts, where ye withdrew to be perpetually face to Face with God, the sweet fragrance of your prayers drew to you your fellows in search of salvation. And soon a monastery, or a convent or a church, rose from the ground. They remain to our days and we offer you this worthy praise:

Rejoice Saints Gregory and Pirmin!

Rejoice Saints Felix and Regula!

Rejoice Saints Exupery and Florinus!

Rejoice Saints Paul II and Wiborade!

Rejoice Saints Candide and Victor!

Rejoice all ye Saints of Switzerland!

Kontakion 6

Voluntary exiles from your native lands for the sake of Christ and for love of His Name, ye came from the green isle of Erin and the isles of the British. From Germany ye came, from Gaul, from Italy, and from Egypt to the land of the Swiss to reap saving harvests of Christian faith, and ye sing aloud to God: Alleluia!

Ikos 6

Travelers of love ineffable, bearing nothing but your faith, bound for the Kingdom of Heaven, ye left on your path the bright shining signposts of churches, cathedrals, monasteries, and convents as ye sang with loud voice to God:

Rejoice Holy Army of Agaunum!

Rejoice Saints Ursanne and Fromond!

Rejoice Saints Amator and Viator!

Rejoice Saints Leontius and Jucundinus!

Rejoice Saints Secundinus and Martin

Rejoice all ye Saints of Switzerland!

Kontakion 7

With the peaceful and simple weapons of the Gospel, ye fought and conquered the paganism of our lands. Then ye defeated and crushed the mortal heresy of Arianism which threatened the Orthodox Church with its devilish doctrine. Ever victorious, ye raise thanks to God, singing to Him: Alleluia!

Ikos 7

Saints of Switzerland, ye form a holy mosaic in which many and varied tesserae are arranged to give your new homeland the blessed face of the Master, full of love and meekness. Wherefore we praise you saying:

Rejoice Saints Innocent and Vincent!

Rejoice Saints Yole and Odile!

Rejoice Saints Gaudence and Gontran!

Rejoice Saints Ragnachaire and Thyrse!

Rejoice Saints Gereon and Victor!

Rejoice all ye Saints of Switzerland!

Kontakion 8

Living in the world ye chose exile at the call of Christ and so became citizens of the Paradise of God. For by your preaching ye freed those who lay in the nets of heathen darkness and the dreadful pit of Arianism. And seeing your labors, the angels in heaven sang to God: Alleluia!

Ikos 8

Tireless pilgrims on the road to the Kingdom to come, invincible heralds of the Lord Jesus Christ, ye led the multitudes to the New Canaan, bringing them to the Orthodox Faith, even at the risk of your lives. So we now sing your praises saying:

Rejoice Saints Protais and Wandrille!

Rejoice Saints Ursicin and Imier!

Rejoice Saints Oyend and Meinrad!

Rejoice Saints Candide and Victor!

Rejoice Saints Asimo and Marius !

Rejoice all ye Saints of Switzerland!

Kontakion 9

Nuns, monks, priests, and hierarchs clothed by Christ with the Faith, in the East and West, North and South, even in peril of martyrdom, ye have patiently built up the Christian Church which now sings with you to the heavens: Alleluia!

Ikos 9

In the twentieth century after Christ, the land of the Swiss received a living saint from far-off Russia. A Slavic Bishop of Western Europe, he venerated the Orthodox Saints of the West. O Saint John of Shanghai, apostle to the dispersed, thou dost sing with us to the saints of our land:

Rejoice Saints Vital and Faustus!

Rejoice Saints Venerand and Achive!

Rejoice Saints Tranquillinus and Ambrose!

Rejoice Saints Ynnemod and Paul!

Rejoice Saints Antoninus and Julia!

Rejoice all ye Saints of Switzerland!

Kontakion 10

Such was the fame of the Christian martyrs come from Egypt, that the whole world over, many towns and villages received the name of Maurice, the commander of the glorious legion which knew how to die for Christ, singing to God: Alleluia!

Ikos 10

Swiss Christianity shone with splendid brightness throughout the Christian world. The blessed martyrs of Agaunum were famed throughout Europe. The faithful came from foreign lands in pilgrimage with many famous hierarchs to the holy relics of the Theban Legion. As they too are holy, we praise their great virtues saying:

Rejoice friends of the martyrs of Agaunum!

Rejoice holy Hierarch of Christ, Hilarion!

Rejoice, Saint Ambrose of Milan!

Rejoice holy bishop Martin of Tours!

Rejoice holy bishop Avit of Vienne!

Rejoice all ye Saints of Switzerland!

Kontakion 11

In the secret chamber of your heart, in the mountains or the plain, in towns and cities, in the countryside, the forests, and on the riverbanks, you were a great company of saints of God who raised your prayer for the Gospel of Christ. And though men knew it not, the angels in heaven glorified you in singing to the Highest: Alleluia!

Ikos 11

O servants of the Lord Jesus Christ, missionaries of His Kingdom, like the knots of a vast prayer rope in the hands of the God of Love, through His grace your prayer has raised, in the blessed land of the Swiss, the harvest of salvation; and we praise you in song:

Rejoice, hermits hidden from all!

Rejoice, secret wonderworkers!

Rejoice, nuns whom God alone knows!

Rejoice faithful Christians of long ago!

Rejoice meek souls of the Church!

Rejoice all ye Saints of Switzerland!

Kontakion 12

The elect ones of God are as the grains of sand in the sea. The grace of the Most-high revealeth a few when they are brought to our minds and our prayers in the Church. But the treasure of the

Communion of Saints is rich in all those other wonderous souls who worked silently in secret, building a rampart of prayer for the faithful who knew them not, and crying unceasingly to God: Alleluia!

Ikos 12

Mystical flowers of the garden of the Church, ye oftentimes flowered unknown to the faithful; but your prayer rose to heaven as fragrant incense and your lives blessed the land of the Swiss through your hidden feats. We thank God for this and now sing to you:

Rejoice holy monks known to God alone!

Rejoice holy ascetics, unknown to men!

Rejoice holy hierarchs whose names are lost!

Rejoice holy hermits whose lives are hidden!

Rejoice holy martyrs forgotten by men!

Rejoice all ye Saints of Switzerland!

Kontakion 13

The fine cross, pure and white, of the banner of the Swiss, on its red background which recalls the blood of the martyrs, is the clear witness of your mission on the earth. For it proclaimeth to past and future ages, the lasting root of the people in God, and through our voices perpetual praise riseth ever to God: Alleluia! Alleluia! Alleluia!

The previous Kontakion is repeated thrice.

Ikos 1

Holy Fathers, holy Mothers, from the dawn of your preaching your spiritual struggle was victorious against the depths of ignorance and the violence rooted in those captive souls, bringing them on a path of light to the haven of salvation in Christ through the sacraments, so we cry to you:

Rejoice Saints Beatus and Achates!

Rejoice Saint Maurice and thy soldiers!

Rejoice Saints Oyend and Meinrad!

Rejoice Saints Sigismond and Clotilde!

Rejoice Saints Tutilon and Notker!

Rejoice, all ye Saints of Switzerland!

Kontakion 1

The land of the Swiss dwelt in the dark depths of paganism, but the Gospel was spread abroad by different messengers, both men and women from different lands; and the Good News of the Light of Christ arose suddenly, as a spiritual dawn, bringing in the new mankind to whom we cry: Rejoice, all ye saints of Switzerland.

Prayer to all the Orthodox Saints of Switzerland

O Saints of Switzerland, pious apostles of pagan lands, monks and nuns who cleared the ground and planted the Orthodox Faith in human souls, hermits and anchorites; together ye form the image of Paradise, where, in the Love of Christ, dwell the citizens of heaven, pious souls of many nations. Pray for us who still abide here below that the Lord may grant us your courage, your perseverance, your strong and firm faith, and make us worthy of being welcomed by you into the kingdom where reign the Father, the Son, and the Holy Spirit unto the ages of ages, Amen!

An Akathist composed for the glory of the One God in Trinity and in honor of all the Saints of Switzerland by Claude Lopez-Ginisty.

The end. Glory be to God.

Appendix 1
Akathist Pattern Melody
Akathist to our Most Holy Lady the Theotokos

Rejoice, thou through whom joy will shine_____ forth:

Rejoice, thou through whom the curse___ will cease! Rejoice, recall of fal-len

A - dam: Rejoice, redemption of the tears___ of Eve!___

Rejoice, height inaccessible to hu - - man thoughts:

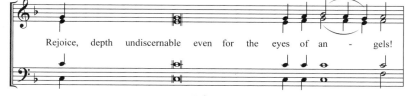

Rejoice, depth undiscernable even for the eyes of an - gels!

At the end of
each Kontakion:

After the final Kontakion,
the triple Alleluia:

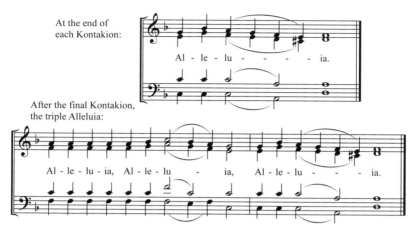

Used with the permission of orthodoxchurchmusic.org

Notes

1   See the biography by Bernard Le Caro, *Saint Jean de Changhaï,* [St John of Shanghai] Lausanne: L'Âge d'Homme, 2011.

2   Please see the service on page 119 and the Akathist on page 127.

3   A collection of the lives of the saints.

4   In Russia, the service has been translated into Slavonic.

5   This date corresponds to the Swiss feast of the "Federal Fast," instituted in 1832 by the Swiss government as a day of thanksgiving, repentance, and prayer for the whole Confederation.

6   Claude Laporte, *Tous les Saints de l'Orthodoxie*, Vevey: Xénia, 2008. We have also taken account of the words of father Macarios of Simonos Petra, quoted by Claude Laporte: "We have therefore preferred to choose the most ancient of the Orthodox Saints for they represent the Undivided Church. Neither their holiness nor their teaching can be impugned. But this does not detract from the holiness of the Western Saints who lived between the end of the eigth and the eleventh centuries."

7   A canton is a type of administrative division of a country.

8   Célestin Dubois, *Histoire des origines et de l'établissement Du christianisme en Suisse*, [History of the origins and establishment of Christianity in Switzerland] Neuchâtel, 1859.

9   Ibid., pp. 11–12.

10 [The Theban Legion was a Roman legion from Egypt of "six thousand six hundred and sixty-six men" martyred in Switzerland in 286 A.D. —Ed.]

11 [Dagobert I, King of the Franks (circa 603–January 639 A.D.) —Ed.]

12 [The Vandals were a Germanic tribe who sacked Rome in 455 A.D. —Ed.]

13 [The Sueves were a Germanic tribe from the Elbe region that invaded the Western Roman Empire as it collapsed. —Ed.]

14 [This is a reference to 2 Tim 4:6–7: "For I am already being poured out as a drink offering, and the time of my departure is at hand. I have fought the good fight, I have finished the race, I have kept the faith." —Ed.]

15 [Swabia is a region in present-day southwestern Germany. —Ed.]

16 [Maximinian (circa 250–305 A.D.) was the Roman
    Emperor from 286 A.D. until his death. —Ed.]

17 [Diocletian (circa 242–circa 312 A.D.) —Ed.]

18 B.P. Dom H. Leclercq Trans. "Les actes des Martyrs d'Agaune," *Les martyrs
    tomes II, le troisième siècle Dioclétien* (Farnborough, England : St Michael's
    Abbey) 1903. p. 171. https://www.bibliotheque-monastique.ch/bibliotheque/
    bibliotheque/saints/martyrs/martyrs0002.htm#_Toc90634929

19 Bernard de Montmélian, *Saint Maurice et la Légion Thébéenne* (Plon: Paris,
    1888). This is a translation of the Latin work by St Eucher of Lyon.

20 [St Theodore, circa 350–400 A.D. (see page 113)—Ed.]

21 [St Martin of Tours (circa 317/336, November 8, 397) —Ed.]

22 [St Ambrose of Milan, circa 339–397 A.D. —Ed.]

23 [St Comgall (circa 510/520—May 10, 602) is known as the "Father of Monks"
    for having trained overfour thousand monks at the Monastery of Bangor. —Ed.]

24 [Brunehaut also called Brunhilda of Austrasia (circa 543–613) who
    ruled the Frankish Kingdoms of Austrasia and Burgundy. —Ed.]

25 [Thesaurus monumentorum ecclesiasticorum et historicorum
    et Henrici Canisiii Lectiones Antiquae (Antwerp, Belgium:
    Rudolphum & Gerhardum Westenios, 1725) —Ed.]

26 [During this time, the mayor of the palace was the power behind the
    throne, as the roles of kings were relegated to ceremonial duties—Ed.]

27 [Isaac served as Patriarch of Jerusalem from 601 to 609—Ed.]

28 [Gozbert served as a deacon, priest, and dean becoming
    Abbot of the Abbey of St Gall in 816. —Ed.]

29 [Pépin le bref (Pepin the short) King of the Franks 751–768. —Trans.]

30 Pragmatius: bishop of Autun (†520).

31 [The Bollandists are an association of Church scholars studying hagiography. Their
    main work is the large collection titled "Lives of the Saints" (*Acta Sanctorum*) —Ed.]

32 [Arianism is a heresy which dismisses the coeternality of God the Father and
    God the Son, attributed to Arius of Alexandria (circa 256–336 A.D) —Ed.]

33 [Clovis I King of the Franks (circa 466–511 A.D.) —Ed.]

34 [An oratory is a small chapel, usually for private
    worship and small congregations. —Ed.]

35 [Childbert I (circa 496 A.D.—December 13, 558) was the third of
    four sons who shared the throne upon Clovis's death—Ed.]

36 This passage comes from the "Passion of Saint Germain the Martyr"
    found in the "bibliothèque suisse au patrimoine" and in Chapter

6 : https://www.bibliotheque-monastique.ch/bibliotheque/
bibliotheque/saints/saints-du-jura/germain/index.htm

37 [Cathic the Duke of Alsace (†690), also known as Adalrich, Adalricus,
Chadelricho, Hetticho, Etichon, Cathicus, or Athich—Ed.]

38 [Randoald is also known as Leodegar—Ed.]

39 Acta Sanctorum. https://www.bibliotheque-monastique.ch/bibliotheque/
bibliotheque/saints/saints-du-jura/germain/index.htm

40 [Celidoine, Bishop of Besançon (†circa 451)—Ed.]

41 [Saint Hilarion of Arles (circa 403–449)—Ed.]

42 [Emperor Charles the Fat is Charles III (839–888),
ruler of the Carolignian Empire. —Ed.]

43 [Adon (†874) is also known as Ado, became Bishop of Vienna in 850. —Ed.]

44 [Raban Maur (circa 780–856) became Archbishop of Mainz in 840. —Ed.]

45 [*The Latin Patrology* is an encyclopedically thorough collection of Western
Church fathers spanning from the second to thirteenth century. —Ed.]

46 The village exists to our day. In the church, the well of the saint
can still be seen. The water from it has the power of curing fevers,
and even nowadays, the saint is still venerated in this place.

47 [One league is approximately 5.5 kilometers or 3.4 miles. —Ed.]

48 [Henry the Fowler was King of East Francia. His plan to be
crowned emperor was thwarted by his death. —Trans.]

49 In 2013 Archbishop Michael of Geneva and Western Europe directed ROCOR
parishes in Switzerland to commemorate All the Saints of Switzerland on the
third Sunday in September, according to the civil calendar. This corresponds
to the Federal Day of Thanksgiving, Repentance, and Prayer, also known
as the "Federal Fast," instituted by the Swiss government in 1832.

Illustration Credits

Mountain range page decoration: stock.adobe.com, ID 257993312, by Save Jungle.

Fig1: Icon, Synaxis of all the Saints of Switzerland, digital image © 2021 Russian
Orthodox Church of Resurrection; en.orthodoxe-heilige.ch.

Fig 2: Map, created at Holy Trinity Monastery; based on Myers, P. V. N. (Philip Van
Ness), 1846-1937, No restrictions, via Wikimedia Commons; https://commons.
wikimedia.org/wiki/File:Europe_in_the_reign_of_Theodoric,_about_500_
(14594568897).jpg

Fig 3: Map, created at Holy Trinity Monastery; based on Trasamundo (talk·contribs), CC BY 3.0; https://commons.wikimedia.org/wiki/File:Francia_occidentalis_pt.svg

Fig 4: "Europe blank laea location map (variant).svg"; Alexrk2, CC BY-SA 3.0; <https://creativecommons.org/licenses/by-sa/3.0>, via Wikimedia Commons.

Fig 5: Map, created at Holy Trinity Monastery; based on NordNordWest, CC BY-SA 3.0; <https://creativecommons.org/licenses/by-sa/3.0>; via Wikimedia Commons: https://commons.wikimedia.org/wiki/File:Switzerland_(no_subdivisions)_location_map.svg

Fig 6: Photo. "Ex-voto du XVIIe siècle de Saint Fromond, ermite de Bonfol." Musée jurassien d'art et d'histoire à Delémont. The original uploader was Alcazar at French Wikipedia., CC BY-SA 3.0 <http://creativecommons.org/licenses/by-sa/3.0/>, via Wikimedia Commons

Fig 7: Wooden Statue, Saint Amé de Remiremont, Charles de Bruyères Museum, Remiremont. Ji-Elle, CC BY-SA 3.0 <https://creativecommons.org/licenses/by-sa/3.0>, via Wikimedia Commons

Fig 8: Photographer Andreas Praefcke. "Mural: St. Gallus" in the nave of the Church of St. Venantius, Pfärrenbach, Municipality of Horgenzell. Public domain, via Wikimedia Commons: Pfärrenbach_Wandmalerei_Hl_Gallus.jpg.cropped.jpg

Fig 9: Photo: WolfD59, Public domain, via Wikimedia Commons: https://commons.wikimedia.org/wiki/File:St_Gallen_Tuotilotafeln_Kopie_img05.jpg

Fig 10: Photo: Davide Papalini, CC BY-SA 3.0 <https://creativecommons.org/licenses/by-sa/3.0>, via Wikimedia Commons: https://commons.wikimedia.org/wiki/File:Columbanus_at_Bobbio.jpg

Fig 11: Photo: Patrick Nouhailler's, CC BY-SA 3.0 <https://creativecommons.org/licenses/by-sa/3.0>, via Wikimedia Commons: https://commons.wikimedia.org/wiki/File:Coire_-_panoramio_(12).jpg

Fig 12: Photo: Milky, CC0, via Wikimedia Commons. https://commons.wikimedia.org/wiki/File:Crypte_Saint-Oyand_-_Grenoble.JPG

Fig 13: Photo of woodcut: Roland zh, fotografiert am 21. Oktober 2010 von der Informationstafel "St. Meinrad - Etzelpass" auf dem Etzelpass, Public domain, via Wikimedia Commons: Woodcut is in the Pubic Domain per copyright terms in the United States. https://commons.wikimedia.org/wiki/File:Sankt_Meinrad_(historische_Abbildung,_evlt._Stumpf)_-_Etzelpass2010-10-21_17-31-14.jpg

Fig 14: Photo of painting "Saint Séverin, abbé d'Agaune, guérit le roi," 1850 by Sébastien-Melchior Cornu. Location: Musée des Beaux-Arts de la Ville de Paris, Petit Palais, Paris, France. Source: artvee.com.

Fig 15: Photo: Martpan, CC BY-SA 3.0 <https://creativecommons.org/licenses/by-sa/3.0>, via Wikimedia Commons. https://commons.wikimedia.org/wiki/File:Saint-Lupicin_%C3%A9glise.jpg

Fig 16: Photo: St Notker, 11th century manuscript. Source: https://inostranka-lib.livejournal.com/7814.html

Fig 17: Photo: Detail from "Sigismondo Pandolfo Malatesta praying in front of St. Sigismondo" by Piero della Francesca, 1451. Source: Georges Jansoone (JoJan), CC BY-SA 4.0 <https://creativecommons.org/licenses/by-sa/4.0>, via Wikimedia Commons. https://commons.wikimedia.org/wiki/File:St._Sigismund.jpg

Fig 18: Photographer Claude Lopez-Ginisty, "Well Cover— Saint Sigismund."

Fig 19: Lithograph by François-Séraphin Delpech, Public domain, via Wikimedia Commons: https://commons.wikimedia.org/wiki/File:Delpech_-_Clotilde.jpg, Location: royalcollection.org.uk

Fig 20: Photo: "Statue de Saint-Wandrille, abbé de Fontenelle." Source: Giogo, CC BY-SA 4.0 <https://creativecommons.org/licenses/by-sa/4.0>, via Wikimedia Commons. https://commons.wikimedia.org/wiki/File:Saint-Wandrille_facade_occidentale_eglise_Saint-Ouen_de_Rouen.JPG

Fig 21: Photo:" Saint Théodule de Sion, Fragment of an altarpiece panel, circa 1500." Source: Ji-Elle, CC BY-SA 3.0 <https://creativecommons.org/licenses/by-sa/3.0>, via Wikimedia Commons. https://commons.wikimedia.org/wiki/File:Saint_Theodule _de_Sion-Musee _de_l_ Œuvre_
Notre-Dame_(2).jpg

Bibliography

— Heilige der Schweitz, www.heiligederschweiz.ch [blog avec une courte vie et une illustration pour les principaux saints suisses].

Anonyme, *Topographie des Saints où l'on rapporte les lieux devenus célèbres par la naissance, la demeure, la mort, la sépulture et le culte des saints*, Paris, 1708.

Anonyme, *Les Nouvelles Fleurs des Vies des Saints*, Lyon, 1770.

Anonyme, *Notices historiques sur saint Maurice et sa Légion*, Fribourg, 1881.

Aubert , Édouard, *Trésors de l'Abbaye de Saint-Maurice d'Agaune*, 1869.

Dom Baudot, *Dictionnaire d'Hagiographie*, Paris, 1925.

Besson, Marius, *Nos racines chrétiennes*, Fribourg, 1921 [concerne le christianisme de la Suisse Romande]

Butler, Alban et Godescard, *Vies des saints,* version française, Lille, 185

Chastelain et De Saint-Allais, *Martyrologe*, traduit en français du martyrologe romain, Paris, 1823.

Dupont-Lachenal, Léon, *Les abbés de Saint-Maurice d'Agaune*, Abbaye de Saint-Maurice, 2012.

Genoud, Joseph, *Les Saints de la Suisse Française*, Paris/Bordeaux/Bar-le-Duc/Fribourg, 1882.

Giry, François, *Les Vies des Saints, dont on fait l'Office dans le cours de l'année,* 1719.

Guérin, Paul, *Les Petits Bollandistes, Vies des Saints de l'Ancien et du Nouveau Testament*, 1888.

Juste et Caillau, *Histoire de la vie des Saints, des Pères et des Martyrs*, Paris, 1840.

Laporte, Claude, *Tous les Saints de l'Orthodoxie*, Xénia, Vevey, 2008 (ouvrage très précieux, avec une excellente méthodologie pour établir quels saints orthodoxes d'Occident sont recevables).

Mallet, Paul-Henri, *Histoire des Suisses ou Helvétiens, depuis les temps les plus reculés jusques à nos jours*, 4 tomes, Genève, 1803.

Martine, François, *Vie des Pères du Jura*, Sources Chrétiennes, 1968.

Murer, Heinrich, *Helvetia Sancta, Seu Pradisius Sanctorum Helvetiae Florum*, 1751. Ouvrage imprimé en allemand (gothique), dates très souvent fausses.

Plantin, Jean-Baptiste, *Abrégé de l'histoire générale de Suisse*, Genève, 1666.

de Rivaz, Pierre-Joseph, *Éclaircissements sur le Martyre de la Légion Thébéenne, et sur l'époque de la persécution des Gaules, sous Dioclétien et Maximien*, Paris, 1779.

Salvadé, Pierre, *Histoire religieuse du Jura suisse*, blog : http://histoire-religieuse-jura.blogspot.ch

Schubiger, Gian Franco, *Saints, martyrs et bienheureux en Suisse*, Saint-Augustin, Saint-Maurice, 1999.

Santschi, Catherine, *Les évêques de Lausanne et leurs historiens, des origines au XVIIIe siècle*, Lausanne, 1975.

Index

147